Straight Talk About Student Life

Christine Dentemaro and
Rachel Kranz

 Facts On File
New York

Straight Talk About Student Life

Facts On File, Inc.
460 Park Avenue South
New York, NY 10016

Library of Congress Cataloging-in-Publication Data
Dentemaro, Christine.
   Straight talk about student life / Christine Dentemaro and
Rachel Kranz.
     p. cm.
Includes index.
   Summary: Provides advice on coping with the problems and pressures
of being in school, examining such areas as schoolwork,
extracurricular activities, and home problems.
   ISBN 0-8160-2735-8 (alk. paper)
   1. Junior high school students—Handbooks, manuals, etc.—Juvenile
literature. 2. High school students—Handbooks, manuals, etc.—
Juvenile literature. 3. Junior high school—Handbooks, manuals,
etc.—Juvenile literature. 4. High school—Handbooks, manuals,
etc.—Juvenile literature. [1. High schools. 2. Schools.
3. Conduct of life.] I. Kranz, Rachel. II. Title.
LB3605.D44 1993
373.18—dc20   92-31488

A British CIP catalogue record for this book is available from the British Library.

Facts On File books are available at special discounts when purchased in bulk quantities for businesses, associations, institutions or sales promotions. Please contact our Special Sales Department in New York at 212/683-2244 (dial 800/322-8755 except in NY).

Text and jacket design by Catherine Hyman
Composition by Facts On File, Inc./Grace M. Ferrara
Manufactured by the Maple-Vail Book Manufacturing Group
Printed in the United States of America

10 9 8 7 6 5 4 3 2 1

This book is printed on acid-free paper.

Contents

1

School Pressures and Problems

If you're like most teenagers, school is where you spend more hours of your life than any place else. It's probably where you meet most if not all of your friends and the people you date—or would like to date! It may be the place where you work the hardest, learn the most, explore the widest range of possibilities, both in and out of classes. It might also be where you feel the most restricted, the most isolated, the most out of place.

Your experience of school may be exciting, boring, frightening, reassuring, depressing, joyful, frustrating exhilarating, enraging, or some combination of all of these feelings. This experience may have changed over the years, or you may feel pretty much the same about school now as you did when you first started going. You may know others who see school the way you do, or you may feel that you are in a definite minority, among your friends, within your family, or in both places.

People's reactions to school are as varied as the individuals themselves. One thing, though, is certain. As a teenager,

1

school is almost certainly the place where the choices you make will have the single biggest impact on your future. And, since you have to spend so many hours a day in school, the choices you make also have an enormous impact on your life right now.

That's why this book exists—as a resource to help you think about all the choices that you have concerning school. Here are some of the questions that you may be facing. Can you think of others?

- whether to stay in school or drop out
- how much time to spend studying
- which courses to take
- whether to get involved in extracurricular activities, like music, theater, or sports, and if so, which activities you'll choose and how much time and energy you'll put into them
- which crowd to hang out with
- whom to date
- whether or not to smoke, drink, or do drugs
- whether or not to join a gang, and how to handle the pressures or threats of a gang that you don't belong to
- how to balance your parents' expectations with your own wishes, interests, and abilities
- how to handle what teachers expect of you

Here are some of the choices about your future that may be affected by how you spend your time in school:

- whether or not you go to college or to some other form of higher education or training
- how well you do in college or in other training once you get there
- what kind of job you'll be able to get, how much it will pay, how interesting it will be
- what kinds of interests and activities you enjoy and are good at

- what kind of experience with friends and dates you bring to the next chapter of your life

So the time you're spending in school right now is really about answering the following basic questions about your life:

- What kind of a person am I now?
- What kind of a person do I want to be?
- How do the decisions I make in school affect the kind of person I am becoming?

Coping with Choices

Choices come up a lot for teenagers. When you were younger, you didn't have so many decisions to make. Most likely, you didn't have a choice about what kind of classes to take, and your elementary school probably didn't have as many extracurricular activities as your current school does. You didn't have as many chances to meet as wide a range of people as you do now, and you almost certainly weren't thinking about dating in the same way.

Likewise, when you were younger, your future as an adult probably seemed very far away. Now, decisions about college, other training, military service, and the kind of work you want to do are suddenly much closer, and the choices you're making every day are much more likely to affect your future.

On an even more personal level, you probably think about who you are and who you want to be in a way that didn't come up for you as a younger child. You may be asking yourself what you think about religion, politics, and all sorts of questions that never used to interest you, or that you used to take for granted. You may be finding that you no longer feel close to the friends that you used to like or that you no longer enjoy activities that used to give you pleasure. You might also be discovering that you don't always act in ways that fit your idea of who you are.

You might experience all of these new choices and discoveries as exciting, a brand-new world of possibility that has finally opened up to you. Suddenly, you can't take anything for granted—what you think, how you'll behave, what you'll enjoy. Everything seems to be changing from one day to the next—sometimes from one hour to the next!

You might also find this time of changes and choices to be overwhelming, frightening, frustrating, or full of grief. All of these feelings are part of adolescence—the teenage years in which you change from a child to an adult. In fact, these feelings are part of any period of change, but since you're a teenager, this is the first time you've gone through this type of upheaval and self-discovery. Because it's the first time, the feelings can be especially intense. Adults going through major life changes—a divorce, a career change, a new period of success, or simply a reexamination of life—experience many of the same feelings that teenagers do, but because they've lived longer and gone through some of those changes before, they might have more perspective on what's happening to them. Since it's your first time, every high and low might seem as though it were going to last forever.

Another reason that the changes of adolescence feel so intense is that your body is changing so rapidly. These physical changes—spurts of growth, voices changing, growing body hair, sexual development—can take some getting used to. They can make you feel awkward or clumsy as you adjust to suddenly being several inches taller, having to wear a bra, or needing to shave. They can also affect the way other people see you and treat you, new attitudes and behavior that you now have to cope with. Your own developing sexual feelings may or may not match these changes in your body and your appearance. Either way, you have both a new body and new emotions to cope with.

In other ways, too, people's expectations of you are changing as you get older. Teachers may expect more work, more responsibility, or more discipline. Parents may expect more help around the house, more planning for your own future, a better performance in school and extracurricular activities, or a financial contribution to the household. Other adults you meet may have positive or negative stereotypes of teenagers that affect their treatment of you. When your own feelings and ideas are changing so rapidly, it can be especially hard to keep up with the changes in other people's treatment of you.

Another part of becoming a teenager—on your way to becoming an adult—is that you start to notice the world around you in new ways. You may be discovering problems that you had never noticed before, or feeling upset about those problems in new ways. Racial prejudice, discrimination against women, prejudice against gay people, the unequal treatment of rich and poor or middle-class and working-class people, barriers against the disabled, age discrimination, and other forms of prejudice may be affecting you, your family, your friends, or your community. You may be feeling the effects of these issues in new and painful ways, or you may be wondering what you can do to combat these problems.

Likewise, pollution and the dangers to our environment, the lack of funding for social services and health care, growing unemployment, and other social problems may be directly affecting you, your family, and your community—or you may be learning about these issues from your reading or observation. You may be asking how you can protect yourself against these social problems, or what you can do to help solve them.

School and Your Choices

What does school have to do with all of these changes and choices? How does what you do in school affect your feelings about yourself, your decisions about your future, your ability to make a difference in your world?

Obviously, there are no simple answers to these questions. Every person must find his or her own answers.

What we can say, however, is that it's up to you to keep asking the questions until you find the answers that are right for you. No matter how you feel about school, chances are that there are some things that you can do to make your choices there pay off better, some actions that you can take to be more successful and more satisfied as a student, in extracurricular activities, and with friends and dates.

Some of you who are reading this book may be excited about school and enjoy going. For you, the question may be about how you can get more out of school—how you can learn to study more effectively, make even better use of extracurricular activities, socialize with friends and dates in even more enjoyable ways.

Others may feel angry, discouraged, or overwhelmed by school. You may have questions about why you should be there at all. Your decisions may revolve around whether you should be staying in school or dropping out. If you're too young to drop out, or if you've resigned yourself to staying in for some reason, you may feel that the only question you have about school is how to make it through until you graduate.

Still others may feel a combination of these feelings. You may find some parts of school satisfying while hating other parts. You may feel powerful and able to make choices in one aspect of school while feeling powerless and defeated in others. Maybe you feel able to choose the classes you want and feel good about how well you organize your studying, but are feeling depressed and isolated from your school's cliques and in-groups. Maybe you feel successful and popular with other kids, but believe that you have no choices when it comes to classwork—it will always be boring, or too difficult, or too much work.

However, for everyone who is in school and reading this book, the fact is that you have choices to make about every aspect of your life at school. You may not have as many choices as you would like. You may wish to take a class that isn't offered, or you might want to be a star basketball player even though you're only 5 feet 2 inches, or you might want to be dating someone who doesn't want to go out with you. You might have every reason to be frustrated, angry, or sad about these limits. But even if you don't like all of the choices you're offered, you still have access to a great many decisions that can make a big difference in your life. And by extending your feelings of defeat, boredom, and anger past the specific things you don't like and on to the entire world of school, you may be cutting yourself off from some possibilities that *are* within your reach.

For example, say you don't like schoolwork. You've never liked it and you've never been good at it. You find every class boring and every test a nightmare. What are some of your choices?

- Learn new ways to study (Chapter 2 of this book has some suggestions on how to study faster and smarter as well as some hints on test-taking techniques).
- Find out whether you have a learning disorder (a physical problem in the brain that has nothing to do with intelligence but that might affect the ability to listen, read, write, or work with numbers), and if you do, get help coping with it.
- Discover some topic that genuinely interests you, such as how engines work, movies and plays, the history of your cultural group, how sports statistics are calculated—and find ways to bend your schoolwork to your own interests.
- Focus on an extracurricular activity, such as sports, music, the school paper, theater, or a student political group, so that there's at least one area of your life where you are learning, growing, and enjoying the hard work of improving yourself (having at least one activity that you care for will make the things you don't like as much seem less overwhelming).
- Figure out what your after-school goals are, and do just enough schoolwork to make sure that you can achieve those goals (just knowing *why* you're working can often

make the work more interesting and less painful, even if the work itself doesn't change).

- Explore the possibility of taking a different class, working with a different teacher, switching schools, or shaking up your schedule in some other way.
- Hire a tutor, either for money or for labor exchange, such as babysitting or yardwork.

Can you think of other things that you might do? Does it feel better to be thinking of the problem in an active way, deciding what to do to make the situation more bearable, rather than simply feeling angry or defeated? Even if you can't change the part of the situation that you're most dissatisfied with, are there any changes you can make that will make your life better? Once again, it helps to start out by asking the basic questions, "What kind of person am I? What kind of person do I want to be? Given all the restrictions and limits that I can't do anything about, what *can* I do with school that will help me get what I want and be the way I want to be?"

Likewise, if you're feeling frustrated, lonely, or depressed by the social life at your school, here are some choices you might have (Chapters 3 and 4 go into more detail about these topics).

- Find a new extracurricular activity to join. Theater is an especially good way to get involved in a group project that brings different types of people close together. And unlike other activities, there are lots of different types of jobs that need to get done in order to put on a play, so just about anybody can get involved in *some* part of the process.
- Learn some new ways of making friends or connecting to people. Take a look at Chapter 4 of this book, ask a friend or an adult that you trust for advice, or observe people whom you admire and see what you notice about how they relate to others.
- Find people or activities outside of school that you enjoy. Having other relationships work for you might have a

"ripple effect" on your behavior at school; it might help you see new possibilities at school that you're missing now; or it might simply help you feel less frustrated with your schoolmates.

- Find a counselor whom you trust. A school counselor, therapist, social worker, or psychologist can help you figure out what's not working for you and what you'd like to do about it. Everybody needs help sometime—maybe this type of help will work for you. (For more on this topic, see Chapters 6 and 7.)

- Explore the activities and ideas that mean the most to you, inside and outside of school. Do you love to read? Dance? Make things? Fix things? Are you interested in politics? Music? Church? A dance class, a political campaign, a church group, a community orchestra, knitting classes at the local yarn store, a local poets group, or similar activities might be available in your community. Or you might start a group at your school to pursue something that you care about. Once your focus is on something other than meeting people, you may be surprised at how many people you meet!

Can you think of other ways to cope with a frustrating social life? It may be true that the people you're thrown together with in your school aren't the friends you'll choose once you have access to a wider range of people. Nevertheless, since you *are* in school right now, what can you do to make your situation the best that it can be? The skills and resources you bring to bear now can stand you in good stead later, when you're in a more congenial situation.

Identifying and Solving Problems

The fact is, even though you haven't created the situation that you're in—being in school—what you do about your

situation is up to you. Even if someone else—the administration, the principal, a teacher, your parents, the other
kids—is to blame for your problems and you yourself are
"innocent," still, you are the one who will feel the effects of
these years in school. You may not be able to have as much
of an impact on your situation as you would like, but until
you try, you don't know how far you can go or how many
changes you can make.

You may find that you can make positive changes that you
never expected, that you can learn to study more effectively
and to get good grades, that you can find a satisfying
extracurricular activity, that you can develop a group of
friends and find someone you like to go out with. Or you
may find that you can build a satisfying life for yourself
outside of school, pursuing your own activities and developing relationships elsewhere, in a way that fits with your
goals and plans for the future. Or you may find some other
solution, some other way of using this time in school to your
own best advantage, rather than simply marking time as you
wait for graduation day.

Whichever way you choose, it's up to you. And one thing
is certain. There is always *something* you can do about a
problem, even if you can't solve it to your complete satisfac-
tion. There is always *something* you can do to make your
life better, even if it's only finding support so you don't have
to get through the bad times alone.

Here's one suggestion for how to face a problem actively
and how to come up with solutions that are right for you.
And here's how three teenagers, Mark, Angela, and Luis,
might use this method to face the problems that were bothering them. (Mark, Angela, and Luis are *composites*—por-
traits of teenagers that combine the details from many
different teenagers' lives.)

   1. **Identify the problem.**   It often helps to write down
      exactly what it is that you're upset about. Some peo-
      ple prefer drawing or sketching what it is that's both-

ering them. Some people prefer talking their problems out with a friend or a sympathetic adult—or even talking to themselves! (This doesn't mean you're crazy. It just means you think better aloud.) Whatever method you choose, find a quiet, private place and come up with a clear, focused picture of what the problem is. Don't just say, "I hate school." Be specific. If you don't identify a problem clearly, how will you know when you've found a solution?

Mark wrote: "I hate doing homework, so I don't do any—but my parents are upset that I'm flunking out."

Angela told her aunt: "I don't like any of the people I know at school."

Luis drew a picture of himself under a thick gray cloud. Inside the cloud he wrote, "Boring ALL THE TIME!!!"

2. **Brainstorm some solutions.** Now that you know what the problem is, stretch your brain to find some solutions. Let your mind roam as freely as you possibly can, wandering from one idea to another. This isn't the time for being practical. It's the time for remembering that there's always *some* solution to a problem, even if it's not the solution you expect. If you're writing or drawing your solutions, get them down on paper as quickly as you can, without stopping to judge or evaluate them. (That will come later!) If you're talking to a sympathetic listener, make sure he or she knows that this is a time for you to just let the ideas flow, no matter how far-fetched they may sound at first.

Mark wrote: "drop out, pay someone else to do my homework for me, ask Pete how come he gets good grades and always has so much free time, ask Pete to study with me, get a tutor, take different classes (*which ones????*) . . ."

Angela told her aunt, "Well, I could maybe talk to Teresa—she lives on my block, and she's nice to me when the other kids aren't around, and she's in one of the popular groups. She might have some idea. Or I was thinking about writing a story for the school paper— maybe I would like some of those kids. Maybe I should just forget about high school—I could check out the youth group at our church. I was thinking, if I got a part-time job at the Donut Shop, I might like doing that . . ."

Luis drew four little pictures: a clarinet (because he had always loved jazz and thought about maybe taking lessons, except he couldn't afford them); a banner that said "Vote for Ruiz" (because there was a campaign for City Council coming up); a bus on a long highway (because he though he'd like to take a trip—anywhere, just to get away!); and a dollar sign (because he kept thinking that anything he would find interesting would cost him money).

3. **Decide how you feel about the solutions you've thought of.** Now comes the time to evaluate. Take a look at the solutions you've thought of—or have the person who's been listening to you say back to you the ideas you've told. Be aware of both your mind and your feelings as you react to each idea. Even if an idea seems silly, is there some way that it might turn into a more practical suggestion? If an idea seems out of reach because of money or other resources, is there some creative way to make it come true anyway? Maybe thinking about the solutions you first came up with will give you different ideas about other solutions.

Sometimes during this process it's helpful to visualize yourself doing each of the things you mentioned as solutions. Picture yourself asking a friend for help or taking clarinet lessons. How does that image make you feel? What would you be willing to do to make it come true? What steps would you need to take? Try to make the details seem real to you, so that you can imagine yourself trying these solutions out.

Mark found himself thinking about asking Pete to study with him. He thought that Pete might be able to give him some pointers. He also thought that if he could combine something he didn't like doing (studying) with something he did like (seeing Pete) that maybe he would feel better about his work. Mark found that he could handle thinking about only one solution at a time. He would try this one. If it didn't work out, then he'd see.

Angela and her aunt talked about several of Angela's suggestions. Angela found herself feeling excited about trying out two or three ideas at the same time. That way, she wouldn't put too much pressure on any one of them. She would go to a couple of meetings at the youth group, and she would try working on the school paper for a few weeks. She decided not to think about getting a job right then, because if the other things worked out, she wouldn't have time, but she felt better knowing that she had some other solutions waiting for her if the first couple didn't work out.

Luis decided that the idea of taking a trip appealed to him the most. He thought maybe he would visit his cousin Ramon in Los Angeles. He was pretty sure he could get his parents' permission to go if he could only figure out some way to pay for the trip himself. All of a sudden, Luis felt like he had lots to do: Check the calendar to find when he would be on school vacation; write Ramon to see if he could visit; figure out a budget for his allowance; maybe think about getting a part-time job to help pay for the trip. Just having something to concentrate on made him feel less bored and more cheerful.

4. **Come up with a plan.** Your plan might include ways of getting help, as well as all the steps that you yourself need to take. Many people find it helpful to write down the steps of a plan. Then they can check them off, one by one, as each step is accomplished. This not only helps to keep your thinking organized, it also helps remind you that every day you are moving closer and closer to your goal.

Mark's plan was simple. He called Pete up and asked if they could study together some time. He figured that he would wait until they had studied together once before planning his next step. If things didn't work out, he would have to come up with a whole new solution anyway. If things did work out, maybe he and Pete could make it a regular activity.

Angela and her aunt made a list of things that Angela could do:

1. Call church—when do they meet?
2. Get a ride—who? (Mom? Aunt Rita? brother?)
3. Look at bulletin board—when does paper meet?
4. Think of story to write.

Luis had started making his plan as soon as he decided he wanted to take his trip. He also realized that he had to call the bus station and find out how much money he needed. Then he started thinking about ways he could earn money. He came up with three: babysitting, home repair work, part-time job at corner store. He realized that each one of these ideas would need a plan of its own. The more he thought about these new plans, the more excited he got about his trip, and the less bored he felt.

5. Evaluate and reconsider. Some time after you've started working on your plan, you will probably want to look back at your original problem and see if your solution is working as well as you want it to. Maybe Mark will find out that studying with Pete helps, but not enough, or maybe it doesn't help at all. He may want to think about talking to a teacher for help—or he might come up with some ways of using what he's learned from Pete in his own private study time. Angela might not like working on the school paper. She may decide that she likes going out for theater better. Or she may love the school paper but still want to do something new to make more friends. Luis may love the idea of taking a trip—but he may decide he also wants some other activities closer to home. Whether a plan works well or badly or somewhere in between, it's always a good idea to take a second look and make sure that you're happy with your choices. After all, who knows what new choices you might come up with!

The Fight for Public Education

As you think about the ways you feel about school, it's good to keep a sense of perspective. Although the laws that say you have to attend school may sometimes seem oppressive or unnecessary to you now, they are actually the result of a long struggle that goes back to the beginning of the United States. They represent the idea that everyone has the right to a free education.

In early colonial days and just after the American Revolution, the only schools in this country were the ones that people organized for themselves. Wealthy people might hire tutors for their children or set up private schools supported by high tuitions. Poorer people in rural communities might chip in to pay the salary of a teacher who could instruct very young children in reading, writing, and simple math. Children from families without much money could not count on learning much more than that.

Some children were not even that fortunate. They were sent to work in mines, on farms, or in factories from a very early age. Either they didn't have parents to care for them or their parents needed the income they could bring in. In the years before mandatory public education and child labor laws, children were seen either as the property of their families or as "little adults" who could be left to fend for themselves.

Gradually, through a series of laws, the principle was established that all children in the United States had the right to a free elementary education. Part of the motivation behind this idea came in response to the wave of emigration from southern and eastern Europe. Universal education was seen as a way to make sure that all immigrant children were initiated into the "American way"—to make sure that they were taught English, the principles of U.S. government, and the ideals of patriotism. It was also a way to make sure that the United States had a labor force that was literate (able to read) and capable of using basic math.

Even at this time, however, "universal" education did not necessarily apply to all children. African-American children, particularly those in the South, were often denied access to the schools that white children attended. The public schools for their use were often of poor quality, given far less money, less well-educated teachers, and poorer facilities. Where white children might have access to education through grade 6, African Americans might be given education only through, say, grade 3.

It took an even longer time before high school became public and generally available. Over the years, as industry developed and the demands of the workplace became more sophisticated, a high school education became more important. Once again, there were several pressures on the government to provide free public high schools. On the one hand, employers wanted a workforce to be educated at the public expense, while many politicians wanted a forum where citizens could be initiated into the "American way." On the other hand, poor and working people, while sometimes suspicious of the government's agenda, also wanted their children to receive the advantages of an education.

In the 1950s, another major educational development took place. In the 1954 decision *Brown* v. *the Board of Education* the Supreme Court ruled that "separate but equal" schools for African Americans were no longer acceptable. If all Americans were entitled to equal protection under the law, then they were all entitled to an equal chance at an education. The Court ruled that separate schools could not possibly be equal; that the same motivation that would separate students by race would be likely to separate resources by race as well. Furthermore, the very fact of separating students by race set up a stigma that made separate schools unequal by definition.

The Supreme Court decision was not enough to integrate America's public schools, however. A major part of the civil rights movement of the 1950s and 1960s consisted of fighting for schools to be integrated. Today, many believe that this process has not gone far enough, pointing out that public schools receive very unequal funding and that this inequality often breaks down along racial lines. Nevertheless, the principle that education is a basic right that *should* be available to all children is still valued, even by education's severest critics.

In this context, it's important to see public education as your right—and, in a way, your responsibility. If you don't believe that your community's tax dollars are being properly used in your school, maybe there is something you can do about it. You might want to get together to talk about this with other students, or even with teachers, who may have frustrations of their own. Perhaps there is a community group or a parents association you can work with, or perhaps this might become an issue in a local politician's campaign. Getting together with other people to do something about the things that bother you is a great way to respond to feelings of frustration, discouragement, and anger.

There is another important consequence of this history for you. Although it was once possible to survive comfortably without a high school education, now, it is not. Today, only the most menial jobs are available to a person without a high school degree or a G.E.D. (General Equivalency Degree, the result of a test that measures high school–level knowledge). Computer knowledge is also becoming more and more important for many jobs.

If you are considering dropping out of high school, we suggest that you check out what the consequences of this decision are likely to be. Who do you know who hasn't finished high school? What kinds of jobs do they have? How much money do they make? Would their employers still hire someone without a high school education? (If the person has been working for several years in, say, a machine shop, a car repair garage, or a shop, the rules may have changed since he or she was hired.) Is this the kind of future you want for yourself—or would you prefer the type of job and the level of income received by people you know who have graduated high school?

Of course, there is a lot that's very unfair about how jobs and money are distributed in this country. You may know people whom you believe deserve a better break—whether or not they have a high school diploma. You may feel discouraged about your chances with or without a high school education, or you may be frustrated at the lack of help and resources available to you in your school. If this is the case, we urge you not to let your frustration and anger make the decision for you. Consider all the possibilities and choose from strength, not from despair.

Making the Most Out of School

This book is your resource. It contains suggestions for how you can get more out of schoolwork, extracurricular activities, and your social life. It also includes suggestions for how you can find other kinds of help in making the most out of this time.

The important thing to remember, though, is that in the end, it will be your own ideas and your own feelings that must guide you. If a suggestion in this book seems useful, take it for all it's worth. If you don't agree with a suggestion, but reading it gives you a different idea, go with your own idea and see how far you can take that. If you have the feeling that nothing you do is working, start looking for the kind of help you need—and don't give up until you get it.

If you can keep focused on your own strengths and on the things that are working for you at the same time that you look for a way to improve the things that aren't working, you will have learned one of life's most valuable lessons. And you will be well on your way to getting the most out of school.

2

Schoolwork

As we have seen, one of the best ways to get the most out of school is to think about the choices you have and to be sure that you are making the choices that are right for you. The choices that you make about courses, homework, and studying will have a big impact on your life today—and on your future. They may help determine:

- how much free time you have
- how you feel about yourself
- who else is in your classes
- where or whether you go to college
- what kinds of job you are eligible for
- how you get along with your family
- what kind of vocational training you can get
- what interests you go on to pursue
- and, of course, what you learn!

Besides making choices about what courses to take, you have choices to make about:

- how much studying to do
- what type of study habits you employ
- how seriously to take your work
- how to deal with work blocks or putting things off
- what to do about anxiety over tests and assignments
- how to behave in class
- how to treat your teachers
- how much extra effort—library time, independent reading, etc.—you will put into a class
- which paper topics or book reports to choose.

In this chapter, we'll discuss all of these topics, first to help you think through the choices about courses and homework that are best for you, and then to help you get the most out of whatever choices you make. We'll start by talking about how school choices might affect your future and go on to discuss improving your study habits: overcoming work blocks; negotiating with teachers; and making use of such resources as parents, teachers, tutors, and the library.

Your Choices and Your Future

As you move into your final year of high school, you'll be faced with lots of choices: whether or where to apply for college, which vocational schools you would like to enter, whether to take "time off" from school before getting more education, what type of job you want to land. These choices, however, will depend on the choices you have been making all along.

Colleges and Universities

Most colleges and universities have certain requirements for both curriculum and grades. However, there are many different types of colleges, each with its own set of requirements. Here is a look at some of them, in order from least strict to most strict.

Public Systems with Open Admissions—Some public college or university systems run on "open admissions," in which any high school graduate must be admitted, regardless of the courses he took or the grades she got. However, the trend is away from open admissions and toward some kind of minimum entrance requirement.

Community Colleges—Two Year Schools Offering an A.A. (Associate of Arts); an L.P.N. (Licensed Practical Nurse); and some other vocational degrees. Most community colleges have fairly loose entrance requirements. They are designed for students who want vocationally oriented degrees, such as the L.P.N. They are also geared to students who want to attend four-year schools but must first bring up their grade-point averages or meet certain course requirements before they can gain admission. Usually, community colleges require the following:

- two years of English
- two years of math
- two years of history or social studies
- a 2.0 or C grade-point average

Some community colleges have a minimum requirement on SATs (Scholastic Aptitude Tests—tests in language arts and math that measure a general degree of skills and knowledge). Others simply require that students pass the college's own admissions test, enabling students to bypass the SATs altogether.

One advantage of community colleges is that you might find yourself being taught by full professors (the highest-ranking professors), since teaching is the emphasis at these schools. Larger universities may have better reputations than a community college, but their professors are under a lot of pressure to do research and to publish. These professors often allow teaching assistants (usually students in graduate school who have just barely finished college themselves) to take over many of their introductory courses. Ironically, you might get more individualized attention at a community college than at a large university. This is something you should research as you think about your plans.

Four-Year Colleges—Offer a B.A. (Bachelor of Arts) or B.S. (Bachelor of Science), required for entrance into graduate school, journalism school, law school, medical school, divinity school, and other graduate study. Requirements in four-year schools can vary a great deal. State or city colleges usually have less strict requirements than privately funded schools. However, some states, such as California and New York, have extensive public university systems, and requirements may vary from college to college. Sometimes, too, the requirements for a state college are lower than those for a state university.

Requirements for private schools vary greatly, with the most expensive and exclusive schools maintaining the highest requirements. Most colleges require a minimum of the following:

- four years of English
- four years of history or social studies, including American history
- three years of math, covering algebra, geometry, and in some cases, trigonometry
- two years of science, including biology and chemistry (more exclusive colleges may require three years of science, including physics)
- a 3.0 or "B" grade-point average (going up to 3.5, or B+, for the more exclusive colleges)
- SAT scores totaling at least 800 for the two tests

Preparing for the SATs and ACTs

Most colleges require prospective students to submit scores from the SATs, although some colleges may prefer or at least accept scores from the ACTs (American College Testing).

Both of these tests are standardized tests, that is, they are organized around true-false or multiple-choice questions to which there is only one right answer, so that each student's final score can be compared to the nationwide average.

Theoretically, if you are passing your high school coursework, you should be able to do adequate work on standardized tests; if you are maintaining a B average, you should be able to do well on the tests. However, sometimes people who do well in class have difficulty on the tests, and vice versa. Even though they're not "supposed" to, some high school curriculums are oriented toward helping students do well on the standardized tests. In some communities, special test-taking courses are offered outside of high school, usually for a substantial fee.

In our opinion, the best way to prepare for the SATs and ACTs is to take the practice tests for these exams. The scores on the practice tests don't count for anything, except sometimes they may be considered in awarding some students scholarships (money to be used toward college tuition). Thus, even if you think you will do quite badly, it's worth taking the practice tests to find out how you are doing. Practice tests can be taken as early as sophomore year in high school, and they can be taken more than once.

In the spring term of sophomore year or the fall term of junior year, students may take the PSAT and PACT, more difficult versions of the practice tests that give an even better indication of what the actual test will be like. Finally, in the spring of junior year or fall term of senior year, students can take the actual standardized tests themselves. Students generally find that just the practice with the earlier tests helps them improve their score on the final tests, even if they don't do any additional studying between tests. Students can take the SATs as many times as they want, but all scores are sent to colleges. Most students take the SATs twice.

For students who want to study or prepare themselves for SATs and/or ACTs, practice booklets with sample questions and suggestions are available. High school counselors or teachers can usually help you get ahold of these practice booklets. (For more on test-taking tips in general, see the section on tests later on in this chapter.)

Attention All Athletes

Students with exceptional ability in sports might be expecting an *athletic scholarship*—financial assistance with college tuition offered by colleges that are eager to recruit top athletes to their teams. If you are such an athlete, you should know about Proposition 48, a recent mandate from the National Collegiate Athletic Association. According to this new mandate, athletic scholarship students must be at least in the middle rank of their classes, academically, and they must be taking high school classes in a core curriculum that includes English, history, and other standard academic courses. (In other words, their good grades have to be in "regular" subjects, not just in business courses, the arts, or shop.) Although this proposition may not be followed by every college, athletes might want to check whether it applies to the schools they are interested in.

Why Choose College?

There are many reasons why a student might choose to go on to college after high school. An increasing number of jobs now require college degrees, even if a college curriculum does not directly relate to job requirements. Even if you can show an employer that you are perfectly capable of doing a job, he or she may not be willing to hire you without a degree—or may hire you at a lower salary. Most jobs in civil service, public school systems, and state-funded colleges link salary and degree in this way.

A student who wants to become a doctor, lawyer, engineer, accountant, or minister will need a college degree to qualify for further study in those fields. Students who want to be architects, nurses, physicians' assistants, paramedics, paralegals, and teachers will need either two-year or four-year degrees. Although there are no formal professional requirements for journalism, advertising, sales, hotel and restaurant management, and similar positions in business, most employers in these fields require degrees.

There are many other reasons to choose college, however. A two-year or four-year liberal arts program can be a wonderful chance to learn more about a wide variety of subjects. Sometimes this further education turns out to relate to job prospects in unexpected ways, for instance, a Russian history major might go on to become a reporter covering Eastern Europe, or a fine arts major might discover a talent for creating new types of computer-generated graphics. Sometimes college courses enrich your life in more subtle ways, helping you to discover new ways to enjoy or understand nature, the arts, politics, human relationships—and yourself.

Years spent in college can be a time to explore the world and yourself before settling down to the business of earning a living. They can be a time to figure out what type of work you want to do, or by what values you want to live your life. They can also be a rich source of friendships, future business contacts, or simply contact with a different type of person than you were able to meet in high school.

Vocational or Professional Training

Vocational training can vary widely. As we just saw, sometimes it comes in the form of a two-year degree from a community college. Various levels of nursing, dental hygienics, biomedical services (such as respiratory therapy or occupational therapy), biomedical repair, some computer training, hotel and restaurant management, introductory business courses, and training in some basic radio and television technology, are generally offered at community colleges.

In addition, a range of institutes and training schools offer specialized courses in various subjects. Business and secretarial skills; cooking; hair styling and cosmetology; radio and television engineering and broadcast skills; acting, directing, and design for film and theater; film crew skills such as lighting and camera operating; classical music performance and composition; fashion design; fine arts and graphic arts; architecture; interior design and decoration; and landscape architecture are some of the fields that can be studied in specialized institutes. (Many of these can also be studied in a two-year or four-year college or in graduate school.)

Finally, a number of unions have apprenticeship programs for training in skilled trades, such as plumbing, construction, and electrical wiring. Sometimes these programs are in combination with a four-year college program that also includes liberal arts courses. Sometimes they are offered as separate two-year programs.

The advantages of choosing specialized training of this type are many. Although many of these skills can be learned "on the job," having some training or background might give you an advantage, particularly in a tight job market. A period of training might also enable you to start at a higher level or a higher salary than you'd otherwise qualify for.

Of course, many of these skills, particularly those in the medical field, are not taught on the job; you need some kind of degree or certificate just to get your foot in the door. Even in fields where you can learn on the job, employers often use the two-year college degree as a requirement, simply to have some way of weeding out job applicants.

There's another reason to consider vocational or specialized training: It's a chance to find out whether you actually like the field and are going to be happy working in it. And it's a chance to really devote yourself to learning your trade, your art, or your craft, free from the pressures of pleasing an employer, meeting a quota, or fulfilling the other requirements of an actual job. It may take you a while to find the employment situation that works best for you, and, for many reasons, you may find yourself working at jobs that don't use all of your talents, interests, or abilities. A period of training can give you some idea of just how great your capabilities are, so that you can hold out for as much as possible in the world of work.

Virtually all of the specialized programs we've discussed require a high school diploma. As we've discussed, the two-year college programs may have specific high school course requirements and grade requirements; the vocational programs rarely do. They are generally not very concerned with your high school grades, either. However, they will want to know that you're able to read, write, and, where relevant, do math at a high school level. Even if they do not set out requirements as such, their own assignments and coursework may assume that you know a certain amount or are capable of a certain level of writing, reading, or math.

Getting Along Without a
High School Diploma

As you think about what and how much to study while you're still in school, you may find yourself thinking about leaving school altogether. In most states, students are legally able to leave school at age 16.

If you are seriously considering dropping out, you should make sure that you're making the choice that is right for you, not simply reacting to a difficult or frustrating situation. You might think about finding other young people who have dropped out and finding out how they earn money, how they pass their time, and what kind of a future they're preparing. You might also consider what kind of vocational or on-the-job training you can get without a high school diploma, training that might enable you to find a satisfying and well-paying job when you leave school, not an endless round of minimum-wage temporary work.

Along with the research you can do yourself among the people you know, you might want to know how high school graduates' salaries compare with those of high school dropouts, nationwide. According to the U.S. Census Bureau, high school graduates earned approximately twice as much per month as those without a high school diploma. The figures went up even faster for those who had some kind of training or education after high school. In other words, the report found that the more education you have, the more money you are likely to earn.

Money isn't the only advantage of a high school diploma. People with those degrees are far less likely to find themselves unemployed than high school dropouts. In 1989, according to the *Monthly Labor Review*, almost 72 percent of recent high school graduates were employed, whereas less than 50 percent of high school dropouts were. Furthermore, all of the *fastest-growing occupations* require a high school diploma. Only a few of these large-growth jobs might possibly be obtained without a high school degree: truckdriver, janitor and maid, hospital attendant, food counter worker, waiter and waitress, food preparation worker, short-order cook, child care worker, and gardener and groundskeeper. Of course, since the trend is to require more and more education, possibly even these jobs will require high school diplomas over the next five, 10, or 20 years.

If you're thinking more of "taking a break" than of dropping out permanently, make sure you arrange your leaving so that you can come back. If you're leaving because of financial pressures, you might think about attending high school part-time while you work, either at night school or Saturday school. You might also consider taking the G.E.D. exam, a test for the General Equivalency Degree.

The G.E.D. is a certificate given to anyone who can pass a test showing that he or she has mastered all of the skills and knowledge commonly taught in high school. Often, tutors or classes are available to help study for the exam. In effect, the G.E.D. offers a person who couldn't finish high school a second chance to get a diploma. However, be warned: The work doesn't get any easier the second time around! What can change is your own attitude, and your ability to get the help you need.

Coping with the Pressure of Schoolwork

No matter what choices you make about the future, as long as you're in school, you still have to face the daily demands of homework, tests, and assignments. Sometimes these demands can seem overwhelming, particularly if you feel that not only your present situation but also your future is riding on them.

Like many other things in life, school can seem like a giant balancing act. You may constantly have to weigh your academic goals against your health, your social life, your extracurricular activities, and your own stamina and abilities. Getting what you want may require giving up something else—or learning how to get help to expand your capacities.

You may also feel under pressure, not just to meet your own goals with schoolwork, but also to live up to the expectations of your parents. Perhaps your parents believe that you could do better if you worked harder or if you just "applied yourself." Or perhaps they don't think much of your abilities, acting as though they expect you to do badly. You may feel that your parents expect too much or too little of you. Or you may agree with their assessments and feel that you, yourself, are to blame for not living up to their expectations. Or, possibly, you take school more seriously than your parents do, so that you want to allow time for studying and trips to the library whereas they are more concerned that you meet family obligations such as babysitting, housework, visiting relatives, or attending family events.

Coping with these various pressures may seem easier if you look at the coping as an activity in itself, a process that has to be learned. For the rest of your life, you will be engaged in these types of balancing acts. Someday you may be asking yourself how to balance the claims of work versus family. Or you might wonder how you can nail a prized promotion when the competition for it seems so stiff. You may have to consider just how hard you're willing to work to get your new business off the ground or to make your demanding new job a success. The choices and means of coping that work for you may change over the years, but the practice that you get now in thinking about these issues will be valuable for the rest of your life.

Freeing Your Mind

The first thing to do as you think about improving your studying is relax! Whether you're worried about staying on the honors list or frightened of flunking out, stop, take a deep breath, and cut yourself some slack. You'll get a lot more done if you can approach your work with a positive, relaxed, optimistic attitude.

If you're really worried about something that has nothing to do with school—a personal crisis, trouble at home—make it your top priority to get the help you need. (The last three chapters of this book might have some suggestions—scan them, or check the index.)

If you feel that your parents are the main source of pressure—either because their expectations seem unrealistic to you, or because they are somehow making it hard for you to get your schoolwork done—take some kind of action on this front. You might want to try talking to your parents, calmly and reasonably, about what's bothering you, or even writing them a letter, so that they have time to think about your concerns before responding. Or you might want to get another adult—a relative, a teacher, a counselor, or some other sympathetic person—to help your parents understand how their behavior is affecting you. Possibly you need to listen to your parents as well as talk to them, so that you can really grasp their point of view, even if you don't agree with it. Perhaps you can all work out a compromise, or at least "agree to disagree" in a way that takes some of the pressure off.

If schoolwork itself has you tied up in a knot, however, here's a relaxation exercise that can help you clear your mind of worry and free it for your work. You might want to make this exercise part of your daily homework ritual, or you might want to turn to it whenever you find yourself feeling anxious about schoolwork. Some people find it useful to make a tape of the following four paragraphs, and then to play the tape as they do the exercise.

Relaxation Exercise

Sit in a comfortable chair, keeping your back straight and letting your hands rest loosely on your knees or in your lap. Your goal is to be relaxed, yet alert and fully awake.

Close your eyes and allow yourself to breathe in deeply. Feel your lungs fill with air; then allow your breath to float out. Each breath should fill your diaphragm—the area just below your ribcage. (You might gently place a hand on your stomach and feel it expand and sink back with every deep breath, to be sure you are breathing deeply enough.)

As you take in each breath, notice the energy and the oxygen flowing through your body. As you let each breath float out, notice the tension flowing out of your body. Direct your awareness to every part of your body, starting with your scalp at the crown of your head and moving down through your forehead, your cheeks, your whole face, and your neck. Keep breathing. Feel the oxygen energizing and relaxing your shoulders, arms, wrists, fingers. Then feel the relaxation spreading with every breath down through your chest and back, down your thighs, through your knees, legs, ankles, and toes. Every time you notice a place of tension, feel your breath surrounding it, dissolving it, and carrying it away.

When you are fully relaxed and alert, slowly open your eyes. Allow yourself to sit for a moment, keeping the awareness of your entire body, relaxed and ready for anything. Now you can begin your work.

Visualization Exercise

Some people also find visualization useful as a relaxation exercise. Either in place of the above exercise or as you complete it, picture a spot where you feel completely comfortable and safe. It may be a place you really know or one you simply imagine. Imagine the space with all your senses. What does it look like? What sounds do you hear? Is it hot or cold? If you're on a beach, can you feel the grains of sand against your skin? If you're in a meadow, how does the grass feel? What smells do you notice?

After you have pictured this safe and pleasant place, see yourself in it, relaxed and happy, enjoying the sense of peace and security. Once you have allowed the peace and contentment of this place to fill you, slowly open your eyes. Continue to enjoy your sense of contentment as you look around your own study space. Then begin your work.

Focusing on Your Strengths

Here's a secret technique developed by top sports trainers. It's more effective to focus on your good points than to dwell on your mistakes. Athletes who give themselves positive reinforcement, even when they've made poor shots or struck out, repeatedly do better than athletes that focus on their weak points.

This form of training is known as *positive reinforcement*, and the interesting thing about it is that it works even when an athlete is having a bad day. For example, let's say a basketball player misses a shot. If she's not using positive reinforcement, she might say to herself, "Boy, that was stupid! How did that happen? I shouldn't have been off balance. Next time, I won't let that happen . . ." In fact, there might be a time when the athlete would want to go back and evaluate her game this way, identifying and learning from her mistakes. While she is playing, however, it's much more effective if she says, "Oh, missed a shot. Well, I really gave it my best. Good for me! I'm really moving quickly today. I'm really putting out my best effort. Focusing on what she *is* doing well is more likely to help the athlete make her next shot. And if the athlete can stay positive even through a bad practice or a bad game, she's more likely to have a good game or practice the next time.

If it works for top athletes, maybe it can work for you, too! Here are two ways that you might give yourself and your schoolwork a boost through positive reinforcement. Can you think of others?:

1. Make a list of 10 things that you do well or that you're proud of about yourself. Post them in front of your desk or carry them with you to keep them in view whenever you study. (If you can't think of 10 good things, ask a friend or someone you care about. Listen and take notes! Then make your list.)
2. As you are studying, make sure you give yourself positive reinforcement every five minutes or so. Silently, to yourself, say, "Great! I just memorized two words," or "OK, that's 10 straight minutes I've been working without a break." If you can't find anything specific to praise, tell yourself, "I'm really getting serious about my schoolwork now," or "Here I am working—good for me!" Try it out for a week or two; then decide if it's helped your schoolwork. What have you got to lose?

Streamlined Studying

Back to the Basics

If you're having trouble feeling comfortable with your schoolwork—whether or not you're getting good grades—you might benefit from a look at the basics. Do any of these suggestions ring a bell with you?

Find a good place to study.   Ideally, your own room at home includes privacy, a spacious and well-lit work area complete with desk and comfortable chair, and storage space for your books, papers, and supplies. If not, you might explore the possibilities for improving your work environment. Would a better lamp, a cushion on your chair, an inspiring poster over your desk, a little filing cabinet help you feel more like working? There are a lot of improvements you can make that don't cost much money, especially if you get creative and if you can find a garage sale or a shopper's bulletin advertising secondhand office furniture.

If fixing up your home space is beyond your means, or if you don't have the privacy or comfort at home that you need, you might think of studying at one of the following places: a friend's house (if his or her parents say it's OK, and if you really do have quiet time there); a relative's house; the public` library; a restaurant or coffee shop (always buy something and tip well!); a local church, synagogue, or community center; in a favorite teacher's classroom, at the school library, or in study hall. Giving yourself the space you need to do your work is an important part of studying effectively, so make your work space a priority until you feel good about where you work.

Make sure you have enough time to study—and make sure it's a time that works for you. If you're a morning person, you might want to do homework before school; if you're a night person, it might work for you to stay up late. However you arrange your time, make sure you've chosen the time when you are most alert and available. Don't plan on getting up early to finish a paper if you're no good in the mornings, and by all means, don't put off studying till the end of the evening if you find yourself nodding off at 10:00. That can be a real setup. Of course you'll keep having bad times studying, if you're picking the worst possible time of day to do it!

By the way, studies have shown that television tends to mesmerize viewers and dull the brain, so if you're having trouble getting your work done, you might want to arrange to do it before you settle down to watch TV.

Eat something nourishing before you start or during a break—but stay away from the wrong foods. Protein— cheese, peanut butter, meat or fish—sharpens the mind.

Foods with sugar—including chocolate and non-diet soda—dull the brain. If you're really craving something sweet, fruit can give you a better lift than candy or a cookie.

Many people turn to caffeine—in coffee, tea, chocolate, and many colas—for an extra lift. If this works for you, you'll have to balance that against all the health hazards of caffeine. However, some people experience a caffeine crash, a feeling of tiredness or grogginess after the caffeine wears off one to three hours later. Other people find that caffeine makes them feel "wired" and jumpy, too nervous to really settle down to their books. If you notice these ill effects, you might supplement or even replace your nightly cup of coffee with some vitamin B, a substance that combats stress and helps promote alertness. (However, be careful not to take too much; follow the directions on the bottle.)

Do your homework drug-free and sober.   Some people claim that smoking a little pot loosens them up and helps them relax into their work. The truth is, they may feel better, but their work suffers. Marijuana may improve your mood, but it doesn't contribute to the logical, focused thinking required by most schoolwork, nor to the disciplined alertness that a person needs to complete a creative writing assignment.

If you're feeling to anxious to settle down to studying, you have several options. You might need to give your attention to a serious problem (again, see the last three chapters in this book if you think this might be the case with you). You might benefit from a relaxation exercise like the one described above or from a good cry or a warm shower. You can also read on a little further for a concrete plan that will help you settle down and make better use of your time.

If you can't bear the idea of doing your homework without drugs or alcohol, you may have another kind of problem. If the very idea terrifies or upsets you, face the fact that you may have become overly dependent on these substances and get help.

Get enough sleep.   This goes for improving both schoolwork and homework. If you feel "blah" and bored a lot of the time, try this experiment: Get eight hours of sleep every night for two whole weeks. No more, no less. (Sometimes too much sleep can be as bad as too little!) Do you notice any change? Of course, everybody needs a different amount of sleep, but if you're getting along on less than six hours, you're probably shortchanging yourself—even if you do sleep till noon on the weekends. If you're used to doing without sleep, you might not even realize the difference that it makes to get a good rest, particularly when it comes to having the energy to do difficult work. Making it through a class or a study period is not the same thing as attacking the work with energy and readiness for some ups and downs along the way.

A Plan for Improvement

If you're dissatisfied with your performance in school, it might help to come up with an overall plan of action. Having an overview can help you relax and take things one step at a time. Be patient with yourself. Accept that you are going to make some mistakes—and allow yourself to believe that none of them will be fatal, as long as you keep plugging away and getting whatever help you need. Here are some suggestions that might help you think about improving your schoolwork one day at a time:

1. Decide on your three most important classes and focus on getting your grade to go one level higher in each. (Doesn't that sound more doable than just "bringing up your grades" or "studying more"?)
2. Speak up with a positive contribution at least once a week in each of your classes. If you haven't been doing so, this will change your image with your teachers—and it will help you to feel different about your own participation. If speaking in public frightens you, find a way to regard yourself after every effort. And remind yourself that practice will help take the edge off your anxiety.

3. Treat your teachers, principal, and other school personnel with good manners. Again, this will help turn around any image problems you've developed—and, after all, it's just good strategy. Even if you feel you're being mistreated, keeping your temper and choosing your battles is more empowering than flying off the handle or acting out. (If you feel you're the target of racial, sexual, or other discrimination or harassment, by all means, speak up—but you might get further by working with a community group or with your parents than by taking the school on all by yourself.)

4. Know the rules. That is, know both the school rules and what's important to the teacher of each class. You don't have to like them, but at least knowing them will give you the ability to choose whether you'll follow them or take the consequences. Maybe your history teacher has a thing about lateness, while your English teacher grants extensions—if he has a week's notice. Knowing these rules could come in handy the week before both papers are due!

5. If you choose to cut classes, choose how and when very carefully. Don't ever cut the first day of class, the day before a test, or the day of a test. Figure out which is your hardest class, and don't cut that at all. It's much harder for a teacher to fail you if you've shown up every day, on time and willing to work.

6. Protect yourself. Keep a careful record of the days you cut class, missed for sickness, etc. That way, if a dispute arises, you can at least make sure that the facts are straight.

7. Always hand in *some* homework rather than none, even if you couldn't complete the whole assignment. For one thing, it gives the teacher the message that you are trying and you do care. Handing in partial homework might also give your teacher a clue as to where you're having difficulty. Also, getting a zero on an assignment brings your term average way down real fast, whereas

getting even a low grade doesn't have quite the same effect. Remember, your average doesn't include just the grades on the work you did, it also includes the zeroes for the work you didn't do.

These two students had trouble with the same work—but Mary didn't turn in two of the five assignments, whereas Gina turned in even her unfinished work.

	Mary	_Gina_
	75	75
	0	40
	60	60
	0	45
	70	70
Total:	205	310
Average:	41	62

If 60 were the cutoff point, Gina would pass, while Mary would fail, just because of those two assignments.

8. Improve your neatness any way you can. Whether it's fair or not, neatness does make a difference to teachers, and turning in neat work might make an immediate difference in your grade. After all, teachers don't have to read just your paper. They have 20 or 30 assignments to read—for five or six classes a day! The less effort they spend just reading your work, the less grouchy they'll be.

   If possible, do any assignment over one page long on a typewriter or computer. Certainly any papers over five pages will be far easier to read if they are typed. If you don't have access to a typewriter or computer, see if you can find a way to pay someone else to type your work—even if you have to offer a labor exchange in place of money.

9. Improve your mechanics—spelling, punctuation, grammar—any way you can. Right or wrong, many readers get more hung up on correctness than on content—and sad to say, teachers are no exception.

If commas drive you crazy and spelling is just not your strong suit, don't despair. You can always try showing rough drafts of your work to your teacher before the assignment is due. Many teachers appreciate the chance to look at your work early, so that they can make comments and suggestions and be sure that you're on the right track for the assignment. You can also ask for help with mechanics at this time, if your teacher doesn't automatically make the corrections.

10. Develop a network of resource people to help you. Is there a friend you'd like to study with? A good student whom you can ask for advice? Do you know a friendly librarian, a smart relative, even a sympathetic older brother or sister who knows the ropes? Even the most successful college professors have colleagues whom they show their writing to, discuss ideas with, and ask for suggestions from. You can create your own circle of helpers too. If you're not used to thinking about your work in this way, it might take some effort—but it will be worth it.

11. Last but not least, do everything you can to work *with* your teachers, not against them. It's easy to feel that a teacher is "out to get you" or "just doesn't care." It may be harder to remember that teachers are people, too, and that they are often overworked, underpaid, and under pressures of their own.

Sometimes, the best thing you can do in a difficult class is to approach a teacher honestly, explain that you're having problems, and ask his or her help to come up with a plan to work things out. Perhaps the teacher can help you figure out where you've been having difficulties understanding or completing the work. Perhaps he or she can help you develop a work plan, find a tutor, or connect to a "study buddy" from your class. An overworked teacher with a large class may not think to offer this kind of help but may be very willing to help a student who asks for it. After all, getting a good education is your right. If you're willing to do your part, a teacher should be willing to meet you halfway.

Of course, some teachers *can* be unfair or unreasonable. You may need to identify these teachers and find ways of working around them. Some of the ways we've outlined in this section may help you there. But before writing a teacher off, you might give him or her a chance to give you the help—and the education—that you need. You may be surprised at how receptive a teacher might be once you show that you are receptive, too. (If you believe that a teacher is expressing prejudice against you based on race, religion, national origin, gender, or sexual preference, you have a right to take action to correct the situation. Find a sympathetic adult to help you, contact a community organization, or look at the resource section in the back of this book.)

Studying Smarter

A lot of people think that if they're going to improve their school performance, they have to study longer. This *may* be true, but it's more likely that you have to study *smarter*. Once you know how to get the most out of your study time, you can make the same amount of time pay off in increased understanding—and higher grades.

Homework Hints

The first thing to know about homework is why your teacher is giving it. That will help you know how to approach doing the work.

It's true that some teachers do give homework as punishment, but usually they have other reasons. Some teachers give homework simply because they think they're supposed to. You can tell these teachers because their assignments are never very hard (although they may be long), and their homework is sometimes not graded or collected. You can save this homework for last unless there's something about the work that you don't understand.

Other teachers assign homework to make sure that their students are really understanding the work. Math homework tends to be of this type. A teacher will assign some of each type of problem that is being studied in class. A history or English teacher might assign a brief paper or give out a list of short essay questions to answer in the same spirit, to make sure that students are following the concepts being taught in the class.

If your homework falls into this category, make sure you do at least some of each kind of problem or answer at least the main idea of every question. If your teacher is assigning papers in this spirit, your work on the first one is especially important. It will help to form the teacher's impression of you for the rest of the semester. It would be worth your while to go to the teacher for extra help on this first paper, especially if you're really not sure of what is being taught.

A third type of homework is assigned as a way of extending the work done in class. Perhaps your history teacher covers the basic dates of the Civil War in class—but assigns outside reading and a brief report on slavery as homework. Or maybe your English teacher has a class discussion on the theme of a novel, and then asks you to write a report on your favorite character. You should at least do enough of this kind of homework to demonstrate—to the teacher and yourself— that you understand the new ideas.

Finally, some teachers assign outside projects to make up part of your grade. They have you do research, reports, or an oral presentation in addition to a final exam and class discussion. To complete this type of homework successfully, it helps to come up with a plan of work, so that you don't leave things till the last minute.

Tips for Better Reading

One of the most frequent ways that students get hung up on homework is through their frustration with reading. But take heart, just as you once learned to read, you can now learn to read better. The following suggestions can help you to make the most efficient use of your reading time while getting the most out of what you read. You may find that all of these are helpful—or that only some of them are.

1. Start every reading assignment by skimming. *Skimming* is the process of quickly looking over a page or a group of pages, trying to get the main idea. If you were assigned this chapter as homework, for example, you might quickly glance over each page, noticing the things that leap out to meet your eye. Probably you would read the various subheadings, noticing that the first part of the chapter is about your future and the different types of training you could get after high school; the next section is about "freeing your mind" and includes various types of exercises; and that this section is about doing homework, studying, and reading. You would also notice that some of the headings—those in the largest type— are more general than the others, which are in smaller type. This overview would help you know what to expect from your reading and would help you sort out the chapter's main ideas from its details.

Besides noticing the headlines, you might dip into the book at various places, reading the first or last sentences of a paragraph here and there. As you find key words and phrases, you get an even better grip on the material's main idea. Keep a special lookout for sentences that start with "Therefore," "In conclusion," "To summarize," or "The most important . . ."

If you are looking for particular types of information, such as for a research report, then you might try *scanning*. Let's say you wanted to do a short report on options for students with high school diplomas, and your teacher or librarian recommended this book. Would you have to read the whole thing? Not if you glanced quickly over the table of contents and noticed all the different chapter headings. That would tell you that this chapter will deal with homework, studying, and schoolwork in general and won't deal with extracurricular activities, social life, or family problems. that way, you could take a guess that this chapter is the one most likely to have information about life after high school. Then you'd check out your guess by glancing quickly over this chapter. If you didn't find any headings that seemed to be about college and vocational training, you might check out a different chapter. If you did find headings on that topic, you could just read that part of the chapter, knowing that the rest of the book would not give you useful information for your report.

By the way, skimming is the most useful way to start preparing for a test. If you are behind in your reading and you have only one night left to get it done, do not start by trying to read every word of an impossibly long assignment. Instead, skim all of the material, noticing what the major and minor ideas are. Then go back and read it word by word. That way, even if you don't finish, at least you'll have a sense of the main ideas.

2. Make a map of what you read.   When you drive your car or your bike down a road, do you pay equal attention to everything? Do you notice the curtains in the yellow house on the corner as much as you notice the street sign that says "Stop" or "One Way" or "Elm Street?" If you're a good driver, probably not! You've trained yourself to pick out the most important pieces of information and to focus on them.

Making yourself a "map" as you read is one way of helping yourself identify and remember the main ideas of your reading. If you are reading a book you own, you might underline or highlight key ideas as you come to them. (That's also helpful for studying later, when you can go back and read only the underlined or highlighted words and sentences!) If you are reading a textbook or a library book, you might take notes on key ideas, writing down each main point as you come to it. Headings and subheadings are often good clues; you might make sure to write down at least one idea for each of them. Or you might jot down one phrase for every paragraph you read, then go back and put a star by the most important ideas.

Some people are more comfortable drawing pictures or diagrams than taking notes in words only. For example, if you're reading about the causes of the Civil War, you might arrange each main cause in a circle, each with an arrow pointing to the center, where you write "WAR!!!" You might need to experiment a little to find the way of note-taking—or "map-making"—that works best for you.

3. Make sure you're not "vocalizing" or "subvocalizing." Most of us learn to read by reading aloud. Some of us unconsciously keep that habit going by saying each word quietly ("vocalizing") or starting to say it, deep down in the throat ("subvocalizing"). Since eyes can move over a page far more quickly than the voice can form words, this slows down reading.

If you think this might be your problem, check it out. Place your hand lightly over your throat and notice whether you feel a slight vibration as you read. If you do, the solution is simple: Chew gum while you read. Since you can't talk and chew gum at the same time, you'll automatically stop vocalizing—and your reading speed will improve!

4. Monitor yourself while you read. Have you ever found that you've read several pages—and you have no idea at all of what you've just read? Or do you find yourself reading the same sentence over and over without understanding it? Doing these things can make reading a frustrating experience. But it doesn't have to be. The solution is to check yourself out as you read, making sure you are getting everything you need to understand the work and move on.

Ask yourself questions as you read. For example, if you're reading about how Native American peoples responded to the westward expansion of the settlers, you might think, "I wonder if they fought back?" Then you keep reading to answer your question—which will lead you to another question. "Oh, sometimes they did, and sometimes they didn't. I wonder what happened when they didn't. Oh, I see, sometimes they were forced to go to other parts of the country. What would be an example of that? Here's one—the Trail of Tears." Asking and answering your own questions through reading will help keep your mind alert.

Sometimes, if a passage is really hanging you up, it does help to read it aloud. You might want to ask and answer your own questions aloud at the same time. Or you might want to rephrase each sentence in your own words.

THE BOOK: "One of the major problems in our economy is called *inflation*."

YOU: "OK. Inflation—big problem."

THE BOOK: "Inflation is the word for that troublesome situation in which the prices of goods and services are going up at a far faster rate than the level of real wages."

YOU: "Prices—what things cost—are going up. But wages—the money people earn—isn't going up as fast. (What are 'real' wages, I wonder?)"

THE BOOK: "Thus members of the workforce have to labor more hours each week in order to be able to purchase the same items."

YOU: "So people who are working have to work more hours in order to buy the same stuff. OK, so inflation is when prices are going up so fast that you can't afford to buy the same things for your same old paycheck. Got it."

Obviously, this type of reading takes much longer than simply reading to yourself, but it's worth it to help you untangle a difficult passage or to bring your wandering mind back to the work at hand. If you feel that this is in fact the only way you can follow what you read, you might skim an entire assignment, note the places that you think are the most important, and read them in this way. You might also jot down a few notes for every main idea, so that afterward you can review your own notes, which should be easier to read than the text itself.

5. Find other resources. If you're having trouble reading on the page, maybe you can find someone to read aloud to you. You may be one of those people who takes in information better though the ears than through the eyes. Possibly a friend or relative would be willing to read some of your work to you. Maybe you could do some housework chores while another member of your household reads to you. Some books—mainly novels and plays—are available on tape; your librarian may be able to help.

You might find it helpful to ask a friend or an adult to tell you the plot of a novel or the main idea of a textbook chapter. A sympathetic teacher or an older student might be willing to summarize the material for you before you read it, so that you have an easier time following the words on the page. You can often buy summaries of famous books— again, usually novels—although reading the summary is not a substitute for reading the book itself.

If you can get hold of a tape recorder, you might make oral, taped notes while reading, rather than writing anything down. Then play back your notes and study by listening, rather than by doing more reading.

6. Go easy on yourself. If you're having an especially difficult time with reading a particular passage, force yourself to stay with it for 15 minutes—with the promise of a 10-minute break to come afterward. If you've got more than one assignment, you might switch from a harder one to an easier one before returning to the harder material. Find ways to reward yourself for working, rather than beating yourself up for what you *can't* do. And remember to keep giving yourself positive reinforcement!

7. Read more—and more of what you like. If you want to improve your reading, and you don't want to be in a special class, one solution is simply to read more. Find out what you like to read, and read it! You can often find books that tell the stories of your favorite movies. You might enjoy horror stories, science fiction, romance, or fantasy. You might want to find out more about TV actors (check out the gossip magazines), dirt bikes (there are special magazines about those, too), or unsolved crimes (ask your librarian *and* your magazine sales clerk!). The more reading you do because *you* want to, the more your reading will improve.

8. Find a reading teacher. You might be able to get tutoring or special help through your school. You might have to advertise and find one on your own. If you can't afford to pay for your lessons, you might swap housework, yardwork, or some other kind of labor for the teacher's time. Be creative! If you're really determined to solve your reading problem, don't give up until you've come up with a way that works for you.

More Study Helpers

If your math homework is giving you trouble, try turning your paper sideways and using the ruled lines to keep your columns straight. You might also buy some graph paper to help you line your numbers up.

Consider ways of working on a computer—possibly at school, at the public library, or at a friend's house. There are two major advantages to composing your written work on a computer: You can make changes very easily, and you can always print out a neat copy of your work. Particularly if you're feeling frustrated with your writing, you might check out the improvements a computer might make. (You can also find a computer program to help you check your spelling!)

Learning Disorders

If you've given all these suggestions a fair try and still feel that you're beating your head against the wall when it comes to reading, you may have a learning disorder of some kind. A learning disorder has nothing to do with intelligence. A person with a learning disorder may be able to reason, to come up with new ideas, and to be creative, but some function in the brain is not working properly, which creates mysterious difficulties in some areas.

One common learning disorder is dyslexia, in which a person sees letters in the reverse order from which they actually appear. To someone with dyslexia, "tab" may appear as "bat." Another common learning disorder has to do with sequencing—putting things in the proper order. A person with this disorder may have to think very carefully each time he or she tries to put things in numerical or alphabetical order, whereas to someone without the disorder, this process becomes automatic. Still other learning disorders can give a person difficulty with recognizing shapes or patterns, trouble with understanding directions, problems in relating oral information to written information (a special problem if your teacher is giving you oral directions to a written test!), or other types of difficulties with reading, writing, and neatness.

Of course, everyone has trouble with something. No one's brain is equipped to be equally good at everything! Most of us learn how to take advantage of the things that come easily to us and how to work hard at the things that don't. But many people with learning disorders have come to believe that they are "stupid" or "lazy" because the things that seem to come so easily to others are so difficult for them. Since learning disorders have nothing to do with intelligence, there's no way to tell you have one except through testing by an expert in the field.

If you believe you might have a learning disorder, find a guidance counselor or teacher who can help you find out more. If you do have this type of difficulty, you can get assistance in learning new ways of reading and working with numbers that will help you combat the effects of the disorder. You can also work with your teachers so that they can take account of your difficulty. For example, they may decide that you should always have written directions for a written test, or that you could use a tutor's help for problems with reading.

Other Disabilities

If you are a disabled student—with hearing, speech, or sight impairment, or wheelchair-bound—the most important thing to remember is not to give up. Getting an education may be more of a struggle for you than for other students, but it can be done.

Public policy in the United States guarantees that all students, regardless of their physical or mental abilities, are entitled to get the education suited to their needs. If you are living in an underfunded school district, you may see this as more of a theory than reality, but you should be aware that resources to support your education are your right—not a special privilege. If you need notetakers, sign-language interpreters, access to school facilities, or other types of support, it is the school's responsibility to provide them to you. You may want to work with your parents, with a community group, or with one of the organizations listed in Chapter 7 of this book to find out more about what your rights are and how to exercise them.

Breaking Through Work Blocks

Putting Work Off

Procrastination—putting work off—is something that just about everyone has in common. Talk to any writer in the world, even the most famous and the highest-paid, and almost without exception, they will all tell you that one of the hardest parts of work is getting started.

You know the feeling. You think you should get started with tonight's homework. But you just can't quite stand the thought. You get yourself a snack. Then you wash the dishes, extra carefully. You wander into your room. Then you notice that you never wrote that thank-you letter to Aunt Sue. Right now, even that looks better than opening your history book—that's how far gone you are!

Or you sit down to study, but you can't quite stay seated. You read a sentence, maybe a paragraph, then you think that maybe another assignment is more important. So you put one book away, get out another, and then wander across the room to straighten out your CD collection. On the way back to your desk, you think of a phone call you have to make. Or maybe it's time to go to the bathroom.

Not only are you not getting your work done, you're not really able to enjoy doing anything else. The work is like a dark cloud hanging over you. But somehow, the lower that cloud hangs, the less willing you are to do the work. And the less work you do, the less you believe that you ever can do it.

Believe it or not, there is a solution. Here it is: Start small. If you have a lot of trouble sitting calmly and getting down to work, set yourself a manageable goal: 15 minutes. That's it. You can't work any more than 15 minutes on this one night—but you can't work any less, either. Sit down, work straight through for 15 minutes with no breaks, no eating, no time on the phone, no television in the background—and then stop. That's it. Take the rest of the night off. Be proud of yourself for having completed your goal.

Sound manageable? You may be uncomfortable, but you can stand anything for 15 minutes, right? Try working just 15 minutes a night in this unbroken way for two or three days, maybe even a week. Then, when you're ready, add another five minutes, so that you're up to 20 minutes without a break. Keep adding periods of five minutes, as you are ready, until you find yourself working half an hour at a time. Then you can think about working for half an hour, taking a break, and coming back to work for another half hour.

Believe it or not, this system works! That's because you are working from a positive place. You are reinforcing your belief that you *can* get work done, which makes it worthwhile to keep at it. And you may find that you get more done in that steady half hour than you used to do in three or four aimless hours of studying mixed with procrastination!

Organizing Time and Space

Sometimes just the thought of "getting organized" can make a person feel anxious. On the other hand, being disorganized can sometimes create an anxiety of its own. You don't know when that big math test is, you don't remember when your English paper is due, and you have a sneaking suspicion that you're supposed to give a presentation in history—but you can't quite remember. Naturally you're nervous! In fact, you're so nervous, you can't stand even the thought of studying—so you put it off still more. Maybe if you organized your work, so that you knew what was due when and what you had to do, you wouldn't feel quite so overwhelmed.

We all have our own favorite methods of organization. What feels organized to you may look completely disorganized to another person, and that doesn't matter—as long as your system works for you.

If your system isn't working for you, however, you might want to think about it a little more. Most professional writers and researchers spend years refining and revising their systems of organization. It might pay off if you'd give yours a little attention.

Some people find it helpful to keep track of their work on a calendar. You can buy a large calendar to hang over your desk or use as a desk blotter, showing a month at a glance, with enough room to make notes for every single day. Or you might prefer a pocket calendar that shows a day, a week, or a month at a glance. You might want to experiment with your time-keeping system. But do consider the value of having a written way to keep track of what projects are due when, so that you can plan what order to do your homework in and know when you have only a week left on that big research project.

Office supply stores sell lots of different organizers that can fit on your desk. Some people like to use looseleaf-binder notebooks with dividers to keep each subject apart; other people prefer separate spiral notebooks for every class, with a pouch attached to each to keep loose papers and materials that the teacher hands out. Still other people prefer to keep their materials in file folders or manila envelopes. Again, you may want to play around with different systems until you find the one that works for you. Whatever you do, however, you will want to have a place where you can keep both your own work and the handouts that come to you in class.

The most important thing to remember about keeping yourself organized is that it's *your* system. Whatever works for you, is right. Maybe you like organizing things by color. Maybe it would help to paste stickers of your favorite cartoon characters on your work: a Spiderman sticker on everything that has to do with history; a Wonderwoman sticker on all of your science work. Maybe there's some other way of keeping your work in order that you have yet to invent. Just keep focused on your goal: to be able to find what you want when you want it, and not to forget about anything that you need to have for a particular subject.

The same is true with organizing your timekeeping. Maybe a calendar makes you crazy. You might prefer writing yourself little notes, or posting those detachable sticky squares of paper in key places around your desk. You can buy folders that have spaces for every day of the month. Maybe you'd do well with one of those, so that when you open to the current day, you've got a list waiting for you of what you have to do. Give yourself time to experiment—but don't quit until you've found a way over, around, or through your anxiety about time and deadlines.

Tests

Memory Helpers
The best way to improve your memory is to get to know it better. Find out how it works. Everyone has his or her own style of memory. Maybe you remember with your eyes—by reading words, diagrams, or information, and picturing them afterward. Maybe your ears are sharper than you eyes, which might mean putting your notes on tape and listening to them, rather than reading them, or saying key points aloud to yourself.

It also helps to know a few basic facts about how most people's memories work. Do any of these apply to you?

- People tend to remember what's important to them. If you go to the store without a grocery list, are you more likely to remember to buy your own favorite foods or baby formula for your little sister?

How this can help you: Get interested in what you're studying. Figure out a way that it might affect you or your life—beyond what grade you'll get on the test! Whenever you get a choice about where to focus your work, look for what interests you.

- The first and the last items on a list tend to be easiest to remember. Say you're making French toast, and you're getting the ingredients out of the refrigerator. You read in the recipe book that you'll need butter, eggs, milk, bread, cinnamon, and powdered sugar or jam. Quick—which items on that list do you remember? Chances are, you remember butter and jam at least.

  How this can help you: Do your hardest homework first, so you have the best chance of remembering it. At the end of your study session, save some time to review the key points that are most important.

- It's easier to remember something that is associated with something else. Let's say you saw two movies on video that you really liked, *Star Wars* and *Batman.* You're trying to remember who was the director of each movie. You just can't remember who directed *Batman.* But you have no trouble remembering that George Lucas directed *Star Wars,* because he's also associated with another movie you liked, *Raiders of the Lost Ark.* The director of *Batman* isn't associated with anything else you know, so his name is harder to remember.

  How this can help you: Find a way to associate something new with something that you already know. If you're learning a new word, for example, associate it with a word that you remember. "What does *vivacious* mean again? Oh, right, that word goes with *vivid*—and it means lively." Or you can create your own association with a new idea. Say you're trying to remember that one of Jupiter's moons is called "Io.". You might picture a big eye winking at you from the surface of the planet Jupiter. The sound "eye" will remind you of the name "Io."

- We tend to remember things that are unusual. If you're walking home and you suddenly see a bright red cardinal, you'll remember it, because that probably doesn't happen very often. If you saw an old red car driving across the street, you probably wouldn't remember it as easily, since that's probably a more common sight.

  How this can help you: Look for the unusual features of whatever you're trying to memorize. Then associate them with all the other details. If you're studying one-celled creatures, for example, you might remember that they reproduce by dividing themselves in two.

- Patterns are easier to remember than random information. Think about the clothes you have that are covered with stripes, checks, or polka dots. Aren't they easier to picture and to describe in detail than the clothes that are splashed across with colors in no particular design?

  How this can help you: Look for patterns wherever possible. Maybe you can find two Civil War battles that both start with the letter *A*—Appomattox and Antietam. Linking them through that pattern increases your chances of remembering both of them. Or create patterns where they don't exist. For example, you can turn the planets in the solar system into a sentence that might be easier to remember than the planets themselves: *M*ark's *V*ery *E*xtravagant *M*other *J*ust *S*ent *U*s *N*inety *P*arakeets, meaning Mercury, Venus, Earth, Mars, Jupiter, Saturn, Uranus, Neptune, and Pluto, in the order of their distance from the sun.

Some other things can help jog your memory.

Take notes in class. Just writing down key points will help you remember them, even if you never look at the notes again.

Figure out what to memorize and what you don't have to memorize. If you're not sure, ask the teacher or check your hunches out with another student. Make sure you distinguish between what you have to *understand* and what you have to *memorize.*

Sometimes it helps to take notes on your notes. There's a story about a student who considered cheating. He wrote down everything he thought he'd need to know for a big test. But when he got done, the paper was too big to hide. So he recopied everything onto a smaller piece of paper, using abbreviations and shortcuts to remind him of the bigger facts. The paper was still too big—so he recopied it one more time. This time, he left out all the things he thought he already remembered from the first two times he'd made his cheat sheet, and he used even more abbreviations and shortcuts. This paper was small enough to hide, but when test time came, he realized he'd forgotten the paper in his jacket pocket. To his surprise, when he looked at the test paper, he knew the answers to every question! Copying and recopying his notes had helped him remember every fact.

Of course, we don't recommend cheating. But the effort of summarizing and clarifying what you know and what you think is important enough to be on the test, might really pay off for you.

Preparing for Tests

Almost everyone gets nervous before taking a test. It's a lot like actors getting stage fright or athletes getting keyed up before a big game. The trick is to do what those professionals do—turn your nerves into positive energy that will help you perform well.

One of the most calming things you can do before a test is to make a clear, realistic outline of what you need to know. If there are points on the list that you are already familiar with, check them off. Then you can concentrate on the other points. If you feel that you aren't really sure of anything, put a star beside three (but no more) of the key points that you think will be most important. Then number the other points in order of importance. Nothing is more overwhelming than feeling that you need to know *everything* and you don't know *anything*. Setting priorities will help you manage the material.

Another good way to review for a test is to look through your textbook, reading all the chapter summaries and headings. It might help you to take notes of just the key ideas as you do this.

If you are preparing for an open-book test, you might want to mark key pages of the textbook with slips of paper or those sticky Post-its that can be pulled off afterward without damaging the pages. That way, when it comes time to take the test, you can find exactly what you need to help you answer the questions.

For any type of test, it helps to make up your own questions ahead of time, as you try to imagine what your teacher is likely to ask. When you've been taking notes in class, you've probably taken special notice of the things about which your teacher said, "This is important" or "This will be on the test." Make sure to make up questions about those. Then answer your own questions, and check your work. Spend some time reviewing the things you got wrong, then repeat the process. (It's especially helpful to do this with a partner.)

No matter how much you have done or not done on the night before a test, be sure to get a good night's sleep. Going into a test rested and relaxed will be far more helpful than anything you could have accomplished in that extra hour or two. Suppose you get asked a question you didn't even expect. The extra sleep might help give you just the energy you need to respond to this challenge.

Taking Tests

When you go in to take a test, be on time or, if possible, early, so you don't add worry about lateness to your nervousness about taking the test. Make sure you have sharpened pencils or working pens with you. Don't get involved in listening to the other students in your class. Nothing can make you nervous faster than hearing other people worry! However, you might engage one student in conversation and try to cheer him or her up. Reassuring someone else is often a good way to make yourself feel more confident.

For all tests, listen to or read the directions very carefully. Make sure you know as much about the test as possible: how to write down your answers; how the test will be scored (some questions may be worth more points than others); whether you get penalized more for wrong answers than for questions left unanswered; whether you have a choice about which questions to answer. If you don't understand something, ask right at the beginning.

Before you start writing down answers, give yourself a few minutes to plan your strategy. Note how long the test is. Decide when you'll stop writing and check your work (five or 10 minutes at the end of the test period is a good idea) or start guessing in order to answer all the remaining questions (three to five minutes may be all you need for that). If there are several different questions, each with different points, figure out now how to divide up your time. (A question worth 50 percent of your score should get 50 percent of your time.) Skim the test quickly to get an idea of what you can do easily and what you'll have to think about more. Then start with the easiest parts first and do them as quickly as possible before moving on to the harder questions.

There are three types of tests you are likely to be given: true-false or multiple-choice tests that require you only to recognize the correct answers; fill-in-the-blank or essay questions that require you to supply the correct answers; and challenging tests that require you to explain how or why something works.

True-false tests usually have more false than true answers, overall. Watch out for words like *always, never* and other absolutes; sentences with them are usually false. Note qualifying words like *probably, usually, sometimes* and *often;* sentences with them are usually true. If a sentence has a negative word in it—*not, never, neither*—you might want to rephrase it so that you can tell exactly what is meant to be "true" or "false." Generally, go with your first instinct on a true-false test; it's usually right. If you run out of time before a true-false test is over, and if you don't get penalized for incorrect answers, mark all the rest of the answers "false." You have at least a 50% chance of getting some right.

Multiple choice questions have many more "b" or "c" answers than "a," "d," or "e" answers, especially if your teacher has written the test. If one answer in a test is far longer than the others, it's probably right. Again, watch out for sentences with absolutes—they're usually wrong. And look for sentences with qualifiers—they're more often right. As with true-false tests, go with your first instinct—but make sure you've read all the choices first. If you run out of time, and if you don't get penalized for wrong answers, mark every remaining question with "b" or "c"—you'll have at least a 20 percent or 25 percent chance of getting some right.

When you have an essay test, it's usually worthwhile making some quick notes on scratch paper before starting to write your answer. You might make some notes, number them in the order you want to cover them, check them one more time to be sure you haven't left anything out, and then begin writing your answer. The time you take to write the notes will pay off in a better organized, more complete answer.

If you get a test that asks all the wrong questions, you might do your best to answer whatever you can, then write a note saying, "I'm sorry. This isn't what I studied." Then write a question of your own and go on to give the answer. At least your teacher will see that you did study, and it might mean a minus or a plus difference in your grade.

If you have a problem writing or thinking quickly enough to finish tests in the allotted time, discuss this with your teacher ahead of time. Your teacher may be willing to give you a separate test, allowing you more time. Or you may be given permission to tape your answers rather than write them. Likewise, you might need help in the form of hearing directions read to you or, alternately, working only with written directions. If such simple changes will help you, see what you can work out with your teacher. You might need support from a counselor or reading teacher, but if you think you have a real problem, hang in there. A test is supposed to measure what you know, not how well you perform.

One final suggestion: Find out the right answers for all your returned tests, save those tests, and use them to study for the final. Most teachers tend to repeat themselves as they sum up for the year.

Putting the Theory into Practice

These techniques for improving schoolwork might sound good in theory, but how do they actually work in practice? Let's go back to our composite teenagers, Mark, Angela, and Luis, and see what kinds of problems each of them is facing with schoolwork.

As we saw in Chapter 1, Mark has been having trouble with his schoolwork for a while. He's flunking math and history, and just barely passing English. He can't quite tell what the problem is; he knows only that he hates studying and freezes up on every test. To make matters worse, his parents have been very upset about his grades. When Mark's father sees him going out to play basketball with his friends, he yells, "How do you expect to pass if you're always playing around like that!?" Mark's mother doesn't yell, but sometimes Mark thinks that her sighs and disappointed looks are worse than yelling. When Mark started studying with his friend Pete, that helped some—but not enough. If he wants to turn his schoolwork around—both to get better grades and just to feel better about himself—he's going to have to figure out something else.

Angela's grades are pretty good, but she's always staying up till midnight the night before a big assignment is due or a big test is scheduled. She's never quite sure how much work she has coming up, so she goes around feeling just a little bit worried all the time—and *very* worried when she realizes that she hasn't even started the 10-page paper that's due day after tomorrow. Angela has her own room, complete with desk and desk chair, but somehow, she can never seem to find anything she needs. Plus, her parents don't seem to understand that she's older now and needs more time to study. They seem to think that she can babysit for her younger brothers and sisters two or three times a week, along with doing all her household chores, making dinner on the nights her parents work late, and spending every Sunday on family trips to her relatives. Angela knows she's never going to flunk a course, but she keeps feeling that she could enjoy school more and get a lot more out of it, rather than feeling tense, late, and not quite up to her best, the way she feels now.

As we saw in Chapter 1, Luis feels bored all the time. He has a hard time paying attention in class and can barely make it through any of the reading or writing assignments he has to do. To tell the truth, when Luis reads one of his school textbooks, he doesn't understand very much, and he remembers even less. Luis also finds it very difficult to sit down and study. Whenever he puts aside a night to do homework, he finds himself making his bed, fixing himself a snack, wandering over to the family room to watch television— anything rather than sit in his room. Anyway, Luis shares his room with two of his brothers, so even if he does manage to sit down for five minutes, someone is always coming in and interrupting him. And Luis hates studying so much, he's even glad to be interrupted by his pesty little sister!

Can you think of some suggestions that might help Mark, Angela, and Luis have a better time doing their schoolwork? Do their problems sound like those of anyone else you know? Picture yourself giving advice to each of these students, and then read on to see how your ideas compare with what each of them decided to do.

Mark decides that if he makes a plan for each of his classes, he'll feel more in control of his work. Mark likes writing things down, so he put his plan in writing. That way, he doesn't have to hold all the information in his head and he can focus on one thing at a time, the way he likes to.

Here is the plan he made:

Math—1. Do at least five homework problems every night and turn them in, even if I don't understand anything.

2. If I don't understand what happened in class, ask Pete to show me how to work one problem. If I still don't understand, talk to the teacher before class—ask for extra help and more time.

History—1. Turn in at least one paragraph for every writing assignment, even if I'm not sure about whether I'm right.

2. Find somebody (besides Pete!) to talk to after class. Try out my answers on them. [Mark figured maybe if he talked his answers through, he'd have an easier time writing them down.]

3. Talk to teacher at the end of every week. See if she'll give me 15 minutes to talk about class.

English—1. Be more careful about choosing books for book reports. [Mark thought that if he tried harder to find books he liked, he'd enjoy writing about them more.]

2. Find someone to check my spelling and punctuation before I copy my final draft. (Maybe I could do them a favor—think about what I could do!)

Mark thought that the best thing about his plan was that he had to do only one or two simple things for each class. He knew that if he made a long, complicated list, he'd feel so overwhelmed that he wouldn't want to do anything. By starting small, maybe he'd actually see some improvement, and that would make it easier to go on to do more.

Mark also decided not to talk to his parents just yet. Perhaps if they saw some improvement in his schoolwork, they'd be happier—and so would he. His friend Pete tried to convince him that his parents would be excited about his new plan to improve his schoolwork, but Mark figured that if his plan didn't work, he'd have to handle his parents' disappointment as well as his own. He decided that, for him, it would work better to keep his plan private. He did decide to work on positive reinforcement, though. Whenever his parents said something critical to him, Mark would say to himself, "I am a smart person and I am improving my schoolwork every day." To his surprise, that actually did help him feel a little better.

The first thing Angela did to improve her situation was buy a calendar. Then she took five different-colored marking pens—one color for each of her classes—and wrote in everything she knew about when assignments were due and when tests were scheduled.

The next thing Angela did was clean up her desk. She used some of her allowance money to go to a stationery store and buy some things to help her keep her work organized: five different colored file folders (one for each class), a vertical holder to put the folders in, and a pretty cup to hold all her pencils and pens. She planned to get some more things next time she got her allowance: a holder for paper clips and rubber bands and a plastic tray to hold little scraps of paper and things that she didn't know what to do with.

Finally, Angela got into the habit of taking 15 minutes every Monday evening to make a plan for the week. Looking at her calendar, she could see what work had to be finished that week and what work she could save till later. At first, she found that her plans were very unrealistic, assuming that she could do far more in one night than was actually possible. With practice, though, Angela gradually got better at scheduling her work. Knowing what her whole week looked like made her feel more relaxed—which made it easier to get down to work each night and easier to stay relaxed after she stopped.

Angela also decided to talk to her parents about her feelings. She picked a quiet weeknight after dinner, a night when both her parents had gotten home on time. She showed them her calendar and explained how much work she had. At first her parents didn't take her very seriously. "You're a smart girl—you'll get all your work done!" her father said. But Angela stuck to her guns. Finally, her parents agreed that once a month, she could skip the family dinners on Sunday. Angela knew that wasn't really enough, but at least it was a start.

Luis realized that he had to improve his reading, both in order to improve his schoolwork and just so that he wouldn't be so bored all the time. He came up with a three-part strategy:

1. Every day, he spent 15 minutes reading some part of his schoolwork. He made a deal with his family to leave him alone just for that short time. During that study period, he practiced skimming, scanning, and monitoring himself while he read. Sometimes he talked to himself out loud, reviewing the meaning behind the words. Gradually, his reading started to improve.

2. He figured out that he was really interested in baseball, so he decided to read about that. He went to the library, and, with the librarian's help, he found biographies of baseball players, a history of the game, and a couple of baseball novels. At first, Luis was reading stories for much younger children, but at least it was on a topic that he enjoyed. Gradually, he found himself reading harder books with a lot less difficulty.

3. Luis also decided to find a reading tutor. At first, he asked his guidance counselor to help him find someone, but because his school didn't have much money,

the counselor wasn't able to help. Luis didn't give up. He put an ad up at the community library, offering to exchange two hours of help with chores, housework, or car care per week in exchange for the same amount of reading help. A retired teacher took him up on his offer, and Luis found that it was a real relief to have someone in his corner, instead of doing all that work himself.

As you can see, each student had different problems and experimented with different solutions, until each found the strategies that worked for her or him. No solution works for everybody, and sometimes, even a solution that works for you for a while doesn't always keep on working. The important thing is to stay focused on your goal—improving your schoolwork—and to keep trying out strategies until you get the success you deserve!

3

Extracurricular Activities

Schoolwork may be a major part of school, but it's not the only part. "Extracurricular activities"—so called because they are *outside* the regular *curriculum*—are another important part of your school experience. Extracurricular activities sponsored by schools can include the following:

- sports teams
- sports "supports"—cheerleading, pep squads, etc.
- theater projects
- school paper, magazine, or yearbook
- student government
- school band, orchestra, choir, or other music group
- language clubs
- chess clubs and other clubs for specialized games
- computer clubs
- special-interest groups, such as a science fiction club

Not all schools have all of these activities; some schools may not have any of them. In this chapter, we'll talk about what you might get out of extracurricular activities and how to take advantage of the ones your school offers. We'll also talk about how you yourself might start the activities that you're interested in, and how you might find worthwhile activities outside of school.

What Extracurricular Activities Have to Offer

People get involved in extracurricular activities for lots of reasons: genuine interest, to make friends or meet people to date, to gain status, to impress colleges, to please their parents, because they're part of a certain clique. Most of the kids in your school probably do things for a combination of good and bad reasons. The challenge for you is to find your own reasons, and then to act on them in the way that's going to work best for you. What this chapter can do is to provide you with some information on which to base your choices, as well as some suggestions about choices that you might not realize you have.

Colleges and Universities

Many colleges—especially the private ones—are almost as concerned with students' extracurricular activities as they are with grade-point averages and SAT scores. Although many state schools simply accept all students who have met certain minimum requirements (such as a B average and SAT scores of 500 or more), private colleges tend to be more selective.

The more exclusive the college, the more these outside activities count. That's because so many people want to go to these top schools, whereas the schools can accept only a few hundred or, at most, a thousand students each year. Even if a school sets a minimum B+ average and SAT scores in the 600s, it still has more students to choose from than it can possibly accept. The school has to have some basis for its decisions, and extracurricular activities are a big part of them.

Admissions officers at most private colleges aren't asking only whether or not a student can meet their school's academic standards. They also want to know whether a student will contribute something significant to campus life. Imagine an entering freshman class made up only of science majors with high math SAT scores and no interest at all in theater, sports, or literature. Or, imagine a college class full of drama lovers, with no science fiction buffs, no athletes, not even any musicians. Would you want to go to a college like that? Or would you rather go to a school made up of people with a wide range of interests, people who can participate in activities that can make life on campus richer and more interesting for everyone?

College admissions officers are banking that you'd choose that second option, and so they want to choose students that will help make that dream come true. In fact, if a student has an impressive record in extracurricular activities, they may overlook a lower academic record, as long as they believe the student could keep up with the work at their school.

From a college's point of view, three types of extracurricular achievement are likely to be the most desirable:

1. Outstanding achievement in one area.   Were you most valuable player on your basketball team two years in a row? Did you play the lead in every class play and go on to win an award in a local competition? Were you the editor of your school paper, the president of your class, the first violin in your school orchestra? Outstanding achievement in one area says to a college that you have a strong commitment to that field and that you are likely to bring that commitment to college with you. Admissions officers will be happy to picture you scoring points for their school's team or writing award-winning articles for their school paper.

Of course, a college may not have a strong involvement in your area of interest. Many small colleges have no sports teams, or they've long accepted that their teams will never be winners. Some schools have a strong interest in music; others can barely pull together enough violinists to make an orchestra. If colleges' opinions are a strong factor in your choice of extracurricular activities, make sure that your focus and your college's focus line up. Or, be sure to choose a college that shares your interests!

2. A well-rounded range of interests. This category is probably the trickiest, because it's the most common. Most students don't win prizes for high school activities, so that's not what admissions officers expect from most students. What they do expect is that students will show a commitment to something beyond simply getting good grades.

On the other hand, admissions officers aren't looking for a long laundry list of activities either. The student who writes that he played football one year and basketball the next, wrote a few articles for the school paper, acted in one school play, spent one semester in the band, and helped out on the senior yearbook is not likely to impress a college. They're looking for students with a few strong interests and the ability to pursue them to the benefit of the entire school. Picking two or three activities and following them through will impress colleges sooner than tasting a little bit of everything.

The activities you pick up might be closely related or widely divergent. A student who is on the school paper, writes for the school magazine, and worked on the school yearbook clearly has a strong interest in journalism, a fact that is likely to impress a college. On the other hand, the student who goes out for the swim team, plays clarinet in the school band, and does lights for the school drama club demonstrates a wide range of interests and abilities, which also impresses colleges. Whichever route you choose, just be sure that your focus, your commitment, and your achievements are clear—if impressing colleges is one of your goals.

3. An unusual activity or achievement, particularly one that the student initiated. When a college admissions officer leafs through hundreds of applications, he or she is likely to read "school paper" or "varsity sports" quite a bit. But how often will this tired administrator read that a student worked as student liaison to a local political campaign, organized a schoolwide recycling effort, or helped start a medieval music ensemble?

What about you? Would you be interested in attending a college where your classmates had spent six months traveling in Nepal, or taken part in a hometown college's psychology study, or learned glassblowing from a local craftsperson? The student who has done something unusual stands out from the crowd as the type of person who will contribute a lot to a college campus, if only because he or she has such interesting stories to tell.

Of course, the college's point of view may not be your point of view. You may have your own reasons for arranging your extracurricular life differently. You may want to try out as many activities as possible, as you search for the ones that are right for you. You may be the type of person who enjoys sampling a wide range of experiences, or you may not be ready to devote yourself to one field. Your school's circumstances may have frustrated you. You may love drama, but your school does only one play a year, it's a musical, and you don't sing. You may have family commitments or the need to work at a part-time job, which interferes with your ability to get involved in school activities. You may have many valid reasons for your choices. Just be sure you're aware of the consequences those choices might have.

Exploring Yourself

One of the most important reasons to get involved in extracurricular activities is that they give you a chance to explore interests that can enrich your life. The ways in which you'll be spending your time as an adult may have as much or more to do with your extracurricular activities as with your schoolwork.

You might be looking at a possible career in sports, journalism, theater, music, or some other activity. You might also develop a career say, teaching high school sports, or working as an advertising copywriter, from a related activity. Your activity might turn into a lifelong love of a hobby, such as coaching Little League or working in community theater. Or your extracurricular activities might simply enhance your enjoyment for some other aspects of life, as you go on to love concerts, watch ball games, or read magazines with deepened appreciation.

There is another aspect to exploring yourself, apart from the actual love of a particular activity. Different parts of your personality have a chance to come out in different situations. It's almost as though you get a chance to be a different person.

The part of you that you use studying for a test or writing a paper is only one part of you. Whether or not you're good at the academic part of school, there are other parts to your personality and spirit that you can discover in other arenas. And you may discover resources within yourself that you never knew you had. The shy girl who is nervous at school dances may discover a new strength and power in a modern dance rehearsal or in an after-school gymnastics program. The guy who can't talk to girls in class may find out that he can make whole audiences hang on his every word when he's on stage. And the experience of being part of a group committed to a common goal—whether winning a game, putting out a paper, or putting on a show—may open up new social possibilities for you as well. You may find that parts of your personality that were hidden in the school cafeteria blossom when you're hanging out after practice with fellow members of your school band. Extracurricular activities give you another place to be successful—and another place to try out the different parts of you.

Socializing

There are two kinds of opportunity to meet people through extracurricular activities. One is the simple fact that you come into contact with more and different people by taking part in these activities. Particularly if your school is "tracked" by academic categories, extracurricular activities might be your one chance to meet a different type of student than would normally be in your class.

Also, even if you know the same kids in your activities that you knew in your classes, you all have a chance to see each other in a different light. Working together on a common project is a great way to get close to people. Especially for people who are nervous about talking to or hanging out with people of the opposite sex, extracurricular activities offer a more relaxed and natural way of getting to know someone than in class, at a party, or at a school dance.

Making the Most of Your School's Activities

Finding Out

Before you make any final decisions about what you want to participate in, make sure you have all the facts. Everybody may know about your school's champion football team, but what about other sports? There may be only a few people going out for soccer, but it might be the sport that you prefer. Does your school have a chess club, a radio station, a sci-fi group? Take a look at everything on the menu before you place your order!

You might also want to check out the different aspects of an activity before writing it off. So you don't want to write articles for your school paper—but how about an advice column? Or maybe you'd enjoy doing design and layout, figuring out how to fit the articles on a page and deciding what size and style headlines to print. You might want to draw editorial cartoons, take photographs, or get involved in selling advertising. You might even find out that no one has ever done any of these things before at your school—but why couldn't you be the first?

Likewise, putting on a play takes a lot more people than actors. Someone has to assist the director, hang and run the lights, add sound effects, make costumes, take care of props, and work backstage during the show to keep everything running.

As you find out about the various activities at your school, keep an open mind—and a creative spirit! You might find that your niche already exists, or you might see an opportunity to create the activity that is just right for you.

Getting Involved

Just as finding out about activities is a combination of gathering information and coming up with your own ideas, getting involved requires both give and take. As with any time that you enter a new group, you will want to find out how things work now and what the members of the group want. Your school may hold orientation sessions at the beginning of the year to help new students get involved, or you may have to go introduce yourself on your own. It's always a good idea to enter a group by paying attention, noticing what other people are doing and what they want.

At the same time, you might have your own ideas of how the group could work, what projects it might take on, or of how you could contribute in new ways. Your new ideas may be just what the group is looking for, only they might not know it yet. Look for a way of balancing your own suggestions with the group's already existing way of doing things. If you do make suggestions for new ideas, find a way to demonstrate your respect for the group at the same time.

Some groups are very fluid and allow new people almost instant "insider" status. Other groups require people to "earn" their way in. If you scope out the group you're joining, you can take its own dynamics into account while going with your own individual personality and way of behaving in a group.

Once you've gotten involved with a group, how can you make the most of the experience? Here are a few suggestions:

- Give the experience a real chance. It often takes time to feel comfortable with a new group of people or to get good at a new activity. Once you've chosen a group, stick with it for a month at least, especially if it's an activity you've always wanted to do.

- Make friends with one person at a time. It can seem overwhelming to come into a new group, especially one that's been operating for a while. It can seem as though everyone knows everyone else, that everyone else is an expert and you're just a lowly beginner. If that's how you feel, slow down. Observe everyone in the group very carefully and pick out the person who seems most open to making new friends. You might find another newcomer to join forces with, or you may get to know someone who's been in the group for a while. Either way, knowing just one other person will start to make the whole group seem like a friendlier place.

- Take advantage of all the resources you've got. If joining a new extracurricular activity means learning a new skill, use every resource you can find to help yourself get better. If the teacher or group advisor is sympathetic, ask him or her for pointers. If you know another adult or an older student whom you can turn to, go to that person for advice, suggestions, or just a sympathetic ear for those days when it seems like you'll never get it right.

- Be willing to make contributions and suggestions. Volunteer to join committees, jump into general discussions with opinions and suggestions, come up with new ways of doing things or new contributions you yourself can make. The group you're in and your own personality will determine how soon you feel comfortable making suggestions and what type of suggestions you'll make. But the more you participate in a group, the more you get out of it—and, usually, the more other members appreciate you.

- Remember that everyone has been a beginner and a newcomer at some time in their lives. It may take time for you to get good at this new activity, or to fit in with the other people involved in it. Just bear in mind that everyone in your group has his or her own hidden fears and insecurities; everyone is concerned with doing well, making friends, and fitting in. If you feel nervous, shy, or self-conscious, try this experiment: Go to your next group meeting, rehearsal, or practice with the goal of observing other people as closely as possible. Notice their facial expressions and the tones of their voices, the way they treat others and the way they react to them. Really try to notice them rather than focusing on your own feelings of nervousness or isolation. When you get home, jot down some notes on each person you observed. What did you notice about them and their interactions with other people? Do you have any new insights about them now?

- If an activity really isn't working for you, be willing to switch to a new one. Maybe you don't like writing newspaper articles as much as you thought you would; the writing is OK, but you hate the deadlines. Maybe your dreams of being the next Denzel Washington or Michelle Pfeiffer evaporated as soon as you actually got out on a stage or didn't get the part you wanted. Maybe you like an activity but really don't get along with the people who do it. If you've given something a real try and it hasn't worked, go on to something else. All of life is a search for the activities and the people that we find satisfying. Sometimes we make mistakes, sometimes a situation changes or we ourselves change. Your search for the activities and people that you'll enjoy most is just a part of that larger human experience.

Initiating Your Own Activities

What if you are eager to get involved in some extracurricular activity, and your school doesn't offer it? You still have some choices left: You can find a place to do that activity in your community, or you can organize the activity yourself, in either your school or your community.

Looking Outward

Here are some of the "extracurricular activities" that your community might offer. Do any of them sound appealing to you?

- martial arts classes
- community paper
- local theater (Besides participating in a play, some theaters let students act as ushers, which is a good way to see a play for free.)
- local filmmaker or student filmmakers from a local college
- music groups: folk music, ancient music, chamber music, possibly an orchestra or band
- softball, soccer, or other sports
- political campaign or other public-interest political work, such as to save the environment, to improve neighborhoods, or to fight for civil rights
- soup kitchens, drop-in centers, church groups, and other places serving the homeless
- radio and television stations (They might be willing to take on a high school intern.)
- veterinarian's office (They also might accept a high school intern who's willing to work.)
- hospital or nursing home (They might have a candy striper or volunteer program, or they might just be happy to have a volunteer.)
- folk dancing group
- jazz dancing, African or other ethnic dance classes

Can you think of other local activities that might interest you? You can find out about what's available in your area by reading local newspapers or magazines, visiting the local library or Chamber of Commerce, calling a YMCA or community center, or just asking around. Sometimes talking to one person will give you an idea that takes you somewhere else. Whether you're looking for a particular activity or just want to find out what's out there, your community might be a richer resource for you than your high school.

As you're looking, be creative! If an activity costs money that you don't have, maybe you can offer work rather than money, helping to paint, clean up, or babysit in exchange for tuition. You might discover activities you like that aren't really set up for students, but with enough flexibility and determination, you might be able to find a way in.

Organizing Your Own

If you can't find what you want inside school or out, you might want to organize your own activities. You'll probably find it easier to do this in your school, although you might want to find a way of doing it in your community.

Here are some of the kinds of activities that you might organize:

- a music group with a particular specialty: jazz, blues, chamber music, medieval music, Jewish music, folk music, etc.
- your own drama group, perhaps including even a student playwright and student director
- language clubs, to practice speaking a language; you can also research the culture in other ways, such as eating ethnic food, going to films in that language, or inviting guest speakers from countries where the language is spoken
- clubs based around an academic subject, such as physics, literature, history, or computers; a discussion group focusing on a certain type of book, such as literary classics, science fiction, fantasy, detective stories
- a sports group focused on a sport or game that your school doesn't offer, such as tennis, racquetball, fencing, even ping-pong (club members may have to pool money to hire a teacher or to rent equipment)
- a games group, focused on chess, Go (a Chinese game), or some other absorbing game
- a political group, dedicated to causes inside or outside of school
- your own newspaper or magazine
- your own radio or video production group (if you can find, borrow, or rent the necessary equipment)

Can you think of others?

The easiest way to organize your own extracurricular activity is to expand an existing activity. If you're interested in photography, for example, you might try to expand the school yearbook or newspaper to include a special division of photographers. That way, you can take advantage of the space, budget, and faculty advisor that are already set up. Your activity might eventually break off and become an independent group, but connecting it to an existing group might give it a boost getting started.

If you are starting a new school group, you'll probably have an easier time if you find a faculty advisor. A faculty advisor can help get school resources that you otherwise wouldn't have access to, such as supplies, a place to meet, and maybe even a limited budget. A faculty advisor also gives your group legitimacy, so that you don't have to deal directly with the school administration yourself.

Whether or not you feel you need a faculty advisor, you should do a little research on how to get a group going before you get started. Check out your school's rules, especially if you plan to meet on school property. Often school administrators say yes when they have advance notice, but no when they are caught by surprise. If your principal sees that a new physics club is meeting after school in the lab, he or she may have concerns about student safety, dangers to the lab equipment, and the school's insurance policy—concerns that might have been easily handled if the principal had known about the group ahead of time. Of course, you can always go directly to the school administration to check out your school's rules, but you'll probably be more effective if you go through a sympathetic faculty member, guidance counselor, or even a parent.

Once you've got your school's go-ahead, your next step is to let other students know about the activity you're getting started. The easiest way to start a group is to find a time and place to meet and then advertise it. You can do this alone or after talking to one or two friends who are also interested.

The following notice is an example of the type of ad you might put on a school bulletin board or have read over the intercom system. You might also advertise in the school newspaper or have the announcement read in classes whose students are likely to be interested:

ATTENTION ALL THEATER LOVERS!

If you want to be part of a new drama group putting on a new play by one of our own high school students, show up in Room 314 at 4 P.M. today, Monday, October 14. The meeting will last about an hour. We need everybody—actors, crew, and people who are just interested. See you there!

Angela Gonzalez
Joe Marco

Faculty Advisor: Ms. Ruiz

Here are a few hints on getting a new group started:

- Find a way to let everybody participate. If people show up at a meeting to find that one or two persons are doing all the talking and have already taken all the interesting jobs, they won't want to come back. Make sure you give everyone a chance to talk and participate.
- Have a clear agenda for the meeting, with no more than three or four points. An *agenda* is a list of things that you plan to accomplish at a meeting. A good way to start a meeting is to read the agenda and ask the group if they agree that this is a good plan. If someone disagrees, you can change the agenda to take the criticism into account. Three or four points is a good number of points for a first meeting. If you try to get too much done, everyone will feel frustrated at all the things you didn't do. If you have no agenda at all, the meeting may not accomplish anything.
- Make sure that the meeting ends on time. Otherwise, many people tend to leave before the meeting is over, which lowers the morale of the people who are left.
- Make sure that the meeting ends with everyone knowing when the next meeting is. It also helps if everyone has

agreed to do a specific job, so that when you have your next meeting, you can keep things moving.

It's a real challenge starting an activity of your own, but if the result is that you get to learn or do something that you enjoy, the work will have been well worth it. And learning how to get something organized will stand you in good stead for the rest of your life. In fact, that may be the most valuable extracurricular activity of all!

Making Activities Work for You

Each of our three composite students had a different experience with extracurricular activities. They all agreed, though, that good experiences with these activities helped them feel better about school—and about themselves.

Mark had always liked the projects he got to do in wood and metal shop. He was frustrated that none of the activities at his school seemed as much fun or as interesting to him as that kind of work. Finally, he decided to start his own crafts club. He was lucky in getting his shop teacher to agree to take responsibility for a group of students meeting after school once a week, using school facilities. For a while, it looked as though the principal wasn't going to allow the meeting because she was concerned about insurance costs and other legal problems involved in having students around expensive and dangerous equipment. But when some of the other students got their parents to talk to the principal, she found a way to make the idea work out. Now Mark spends one afternoon a week doing the work he loves and making friends with other people who also like working with their hands. He's noticed that really liking one thing about school helps him feel better about school in general.

As we saw in Chapter 1, Angela wanted to go out for the school paper, so her first step was to find out how she could do that. She asked a couple of other students in her class, but nobody knew anything. Finally, she asked her English teacher, who also didn't know, but who was willing to find out for her.

It turned out that the paper staff met every Tuesday and Thursday after school. Angela knew her parents would want her to keep on babysitting and wouldn't let her take two days a week, but she figured she would go to one meeting and see what happened from there. She waited until she had a free Thursday, went to a meeting, and kept her eyes open. After the meeting was over, she went to talk to a couple of the other kids who hadn't said much. Sure enough, they also could come only one day a week, so Angela knew that she could do that, too.

Her next step was to talk to her parents about getting "time off" from her household responsibilities. She decided to talk to her favorite aunt, Teresa, who agreed to put in a word for her. To Angela's surprise, Teresa was successful, and her parents agreed to let her take the time.

Now all she had to do was figure out a way to become part of the group! Angela continued to keep her eyes open, so that she could see what kinds of stories other people were doing and what steps they went through to get them published. Because she felt a little shy about talking to the real "in-group," she hung out mainly with the other once-a-week people. But pretty soon, after she had published three interesting stories, she found herself giving advice to the next batch of newcomers!

Luis didn't have any trouble choosing his extracurricular activity. He loved baseball more than anything, and, lucky for him, his school did have a baseball team. For one year, Luis was happy playing the sport he loved two or three days a week after school.

Then his school's budget was cut and the first thing to go was the baseball team. Luis was furious, then disappointed, then depressed. Then he decided not to take the situation lying down. He asked all the shopkeepers in his neighborhood until he finally found someone who knew about a neighborhood ball team, made up mainly of men who worked in the local bottling plant. Luis got the phone number of someone on the team, called him up, and convinced the man to let Luis play with them on weekends. Luis would rather have played at school, but some baseball was better than no baseball. And Luis was also proud of himself for solving his problem.

Each of these three students had very different interests, and each faced a different kind of obstacle on the way to finding a satisfying extracurricular activity. What each of them learned, though, was that with creativity and persistence, they could find ways to solve whatever problems they faced. Their solutions might not be perfect, but they were definitely an improvement over feeling bored, stuck, or left out. Do their strategies give you any ideas for pursuing your own extracurricular activities?

4

Social Life

Although what you do in class and in extracurricular activities are big parts of school, who you know, who you hang out with, and who you date are certainly other big parts. As with all the other topics we've discussed, the key to getting the most out of your social life is to keep asking yourself what is right for you, and then finding the courage and the determination to stick to your own choices.

Sometimes this may not be easy. For one thing, you don't always know what you think about people, values, even about whom you like. You meet someone you think is cute, you're all excited, then a friend says, "You want to go out with *him?* (or *her?*)" and suddenly you think, "Gee, maybe they're not so cool after all." You're not being dishonest. You're just not very sure of your judgment.

Or you have a best friend from the time you were in first grade, but all of a sudden, you don't have much to say to each other any more. You want to be loyal and a true friend, but you're really not that interested. What's worse, you're starting to make friends with some new kids whom you really do like—and they don't get along with your old friend at all. It's not that you're not willing to do the right thing— you don't even know what the "right thing" is.

Making decisions about whom to spend time with, whom to go out with, and whom to trust is a big part of adult life. Now that you're getting closer to being an adult, you're getting your first taste of making those decisions. Like any first, this one is hard if only because you're not familiar with it. It's also hard because your body, your values, and your experience are changing rapidly, almost from day to day or even hour to hour. Your taste in food, clothes, and movies keeps changing—why not your taste in people?

There are no hard and fast rules that will tell you how to make good judgments and how to live by them. And sometimes, even if you act in the ways that are right for you, things might not work out. The friends you want or the dates you're attracted to just aren't interested in you. Accepting occasional disappointment is also a part of life.

The good news is that there are some pointers that can help you to come to satisfying decisions and to act on them effectively. In this chapter, we'll talk about ways of checking in with yourself so that you can do everything in your power to have the kind of social life you want.

Cliques, Groups, and "Popular Kids"

Almost every school breaks down into groups or "cliques" made up of different types of kids. To some extent, these groups—such as the "jocks," the computer-science kids, the "artsy" students—reflect different interests. But to some extent, cliques may function as a hierarchy: most popular kids, next most popular kids, and so on, right on down to kids who are considered "the geeks" or "the losers."

There are both good and bad things about groups. Although groups of friends exist at all ages, groups are especially important to teenagers. That's because the teenage years are a time of figuring out who you are. They're also a time of separating from your parents and your family. For many young people, the teenage years are the first time they have a chance to do things their way, rather than their parents' way. Even if you have always agreed with your parents' views before, even if you eventually end up holding on to a lot of your family's values, the teenage years are still a time of making sure that your ideas are really your ideas, not your family's or anybody else's.

How do groups fit into that process? Well, if you aren't going to follow your family's values, whose values will you follow? You may be ready to break away from what you've grown up with, but not yet sure what you want to become. Being part of a group of friends is a kind of bridge between being a child inside your family and being an independent adult all on your own. It's like the old saying, "There's safety in numbers." Being part of a group of friends can help you feel more secure about breaking away from your family.

So the good thing about groups is that they give teenagers a chance to explore different ways of being and to try out independence and separating from their parents. The bad thing about groups is that they can also be restrictive. Because the teenage years are a scary time, groups can often insist that every member behave the same way, just to help everyone feel secure in the midst of so many changes. And in high school and middle school, the system of groups or cliques can work together to keep everybody in a secure place— "popular," "nerdy," "jock," "geek." Although in reality personalities and positions are changing constantly, the system of groups can give everyone the illusion that everybody has a permanent and secure place. Even if your place is near the bottom or on the fringes, it may feel more secure to "know your place" than to challenge the entire system.

What does this mean for you? It means that you might want to think hard about the role that groups and cliques play in your life. If you are part of a group of friends that you enjoy, good for you! These may be friends that encourage and support you, friends that you might even keep for the rest of your life. Compromise is one of the most important lessons to learn in life, so if you're learning productive ways to compromise from your friends, that's a good thing.

But be careful. If your friends are talking you into taking actions that aren't right for you, if you're feeling bad because you don't always agree with them or aren't always like them, if you're hiding a lot of your feelings and your thoughts because you're ashamed of them or worried about your friends' reactions, then you might want to reconsider how you're handling your friendships.

Likewise, you might want to think closely about whether you are compromising on things that are important to you, for example: dropping other friends, giving up favorite activities, limiting whom you date, cheating in school, getting involved with drugs or alcohol in a way that you're not comfortable with, or having sexual relationships that you're not ready for. If your loyalty to your friends is taking you to any of those places, you might want to make some changes in the relationships.

If that's what you decide, there are lots of steps you can take. Perhaps you have more freedom to "be yourself" than you're making use of. You might want to try expressing your thoughts or participating in the activities you enjoy and trust that your friends will accept you anyway. Perhaps you need to make some distance from these friends; perhaps you might also need to see some new friends with whom you can be more honest— or at least share different parts of yourself. You might want to have a talk with one or more of your friends, explaining that you "need some space," or that you want to stay close while also pursuing your own interests.

Making, Keeping, and Changing Friends

Meeting New People

At the moment, your greatest concern with groups may be how to join one! Perhaps you've been a loner, someone who hasn't had close friends or a strong group, but now you're feeling the need for a different kind of social life. Perhaps your closest friends have moved or are going to another school, or perhaps you yourself have moved or transferred. Possibly you were once part of a group but now, for some reason, you're not. However it happened, you're facing school without the kind of friends you want, and you're wondering how to get them.

The first thing to remember is to be patient and to keep your perspective. Being lonely does hurt sometimes, and there are times when it feels as though it will last forever. But there's nothing you can do about "forever"; you can take it only one day at a time. And the easier you take it, the more relaxed you'll be—and the more attractive you'll be to the friends you want.

You might take some time to observe the different groups and the various people at your school and decide whom you'd really like to be friends with. Although the "popular" kids seem to be the ones that everybody envies, take a closer look. Do you really like the way they treat each other? Do you like the way they treat you? Are you interested in what they talk about? If they weren't popular, would you still enjoy spending time with them, just because of the kind of people they are?

If you keep answering yes, go ahead—this is the group for you. But if not, you might look a little further to find the people who are going to be the most satisfying friends for you. Perhaps you'll find them all in one group; perhaps you'll be interested in many different people spread throughout a variety of groups; or maybe you'll want to connect to some "loners" who aren't in any group at all. Whatever your decision, it will be easier to act on it if it's really *your* decision, one that comes from inside you.

Once you know who you want to be friends with, pick out the most approachable person and concentrate on him or her at first. It can be hard to "crack" an entire group at once, especially one that's been together for a long time. See what opportunities you can find to talk to just one person at a time. Do you share any classes? Is there time to talk in the halls between classes, or before or after school? Is there an extra-curricular activity that you're both interested in?

The easiest way to start a conversation is to focus on something that you're both doing. It's also good to ask questions, request information, or ask for advice. Here are a few sample conversation openers that might give you some ideas: "Hi, do you know where Room 227 is?" "I can't decide, do you think this color is right for me?" "What do you think, is Coach Smith as tough as everybody says?"

If you're involved in activities with someone you want to know better, you can always suggest spending time together as an extension of those activities. For example, "Isn't this math hard? Do you think it would help to study together?" "Now that choir practice is over, do you want to go get a soda?" If you are new to a school, or to a group, you may have to do more of the work of getting the friendship going. Once again, be patient. It may take time before people catch on to what a great friend you can be!

If you've tried a few times without success to make friends with one person, or one group, don't despair. You've just found that that person, that group, isn't the right one for you. Go back to observing the rest of the student body until you find someone else you'd like to get to know or some other group that you'd like to be part of. Keeping your spirits up is important, because if you don't believe you're a valuable friend, it's very hard for anyone else to believe it. But if you approach people with genuine interest in them and genuine faith in yourself, sooner or later you'll find the friends that are right for you.

Keeping Friends

The best way to keep your friends is to be a good friend. How do you know what "being a good friend" is? Ask yourself how you would like to be treated by your friends. That's probably a good general guide to how others would like to be treated as well.

Here are some elements that help to make up a good friendship. How do they apply to your friendships?

Each person gets to do things that he or she likes, at least some of the time.   You like to play ball; your friend prefers sacking out in front of a good movie on the VCR. In a good friendship, there's room to do things that both people like. Maybe you and your friend spend some time doing each activity, or switch off from one to the other. Maybe you don't do either of those things together, but find a third thing that both of you like to do. Either way, in a good friendship, each person is willing to compromise some of the time, but no one has to compromise all of the time.

You can do things apart as well as together, and you can each have other friends without anyone getting jealous. Of course, if your friend really hates playing ball, maybe that's something you do with your second-best friend. If you hate those horror movies that are your friend's favorite, maybe your friend watches those with another companion. You and your friend may get jealous occasionally; that's human nature. But each of you know how to keep the jealousy under control, because each of you is basically secure in the friendship.

You're loyal to each other—no gossip, backbiting, ganging up, or ignoring, no matter who else is around. Not all your friends have to get along together. It's even all right to be friends with two people who really hate each other. Just make sure that you never say anything behind your friend's back that you wouldn't say to his or her face. And be sure that you're never in a position where you have to pretend that you're *not* friends with somebody, no matter who else you're with.

If something is wrong, you talk about it and work it out.   Let's say you and your friend are supposed to meet at the movies. You hang around till you miss the first 20 minutes of the show, but your friend never shows up. Later you get a call from your friend, saying, "Gee, I'm sorry, but you know I've been wanting to date Chris, and I ran into him (or her!) just as I was on my way to meet you . . ." Do you have to say nothing to be a good friend?

Not at all! Part of making your friendship work is expressing your anger and giving your friend a chance to respond. Even if you're angry or upset about something that you know is silly, in a good friendship, there's room to share those feelings. A good friend might be able to say, "I know it's silly of me, but sometimes I get jealous of all the time you spend with Chris."

If you're concerned about your friend, you say so—and if necessary, you tell someone else. If you see your friend getting into trouble or doing something that worries you, part of being a good friend is to say something. Maybe your friend is driving recklessly and you're concerned. Or maybe your friend seems moody and depressed, and you're wondering if something is wrong. You might even be concerned that your friend has a drug or alcohol problem, or that he or she is undergoing some kind of physical, emotional, or sexual abuse. The better friend you are, the more willing you'll be to take the risk of talking about the problem to your friend, encouraging your friend to talk about it, or, if you're really concerned, telling a sympathetic adult who might be able to help.

Fighting and Making Up

Many people believe that good friends never fight. According to this thinking, if you fight with someone, you're not good friends.

In fact, the truth is often the other way around: It's only with your good friends that you feel comfortable enough to fight! Frequently, we fight with the people whom we feel closest to. That's because they are more important to us than other people, so their opinions, decisions, and moods affect us far more deeply. You might not care if someone you just met doesn't agree with you, but it might really bother you if your best friend doesn't share your opinion, especially if you feel a little insecure about it yourself and you were counting on your friend's support. You might not even notice if a store clerk is in a bad mood, but if a good friend is gloomy or irritable, that can really spoil your good times together. Who cares if someone you don't like much isn't going to the dance, but if your friend doesn't want to go, that will make a real difference in your evening.

There's another reason why we fight with our friends: They're close to us. Sometimes it can be a little scary to care about someone or to feel close to another person. You realize how much the person means to you, and you know how hurt you'd be if the person left you or stopped liking you so much. Sometimes it seems like the only way to handle this happy-sad closeness is to push the person away before he or she leaves first. A fight can be a way of doing that, a way of saying, "I don't want you to be so important to me—because I'm too scared of losing you." It's a good idea to try to identify when this is going on, so that you and your friend can deal with your feelings in more satisfying ways.

In any case, an occasional fight with a friend means only that you trust each other enough and care enough about each other to be willing to fight! Of course, if you and your friend are fighting frequently, that's something else. You and your friend may need to have a talk about what's going on.

You may find that the fights have nothing to do with what's going on between you. Maybe one of you is worried about a situation at home or school but doesn't feel safe dealing with the worry directly. This worry may be coming out in a safer space—the space of your friendship.

Or you may find that the fights are about something specific, something that can be changed. Maybe one of you is engaging in hurtful behavior without realizing it, such as changing plans at the last minute or making funny remarks that really carry a painful sting. If this behavior is easy to change, then the problem is solved. If you find that the behavior continues, even after you've talked about it, then you may need to look deeper. Perhaps one of you really is angry about something important, and this anger is coming out in hidden ways, such as being late, changing plans, or sarcastic remarks.

Maybe one of you really does want to end the friendship but doesn't want to admit it, even to yourself.

Whatever is behind your fights, talking about the problem as honestly and openly as possible might help the two of you to resolve things. You might agree not to spend so much time together—or you might end up closer than ever! Even if the two of you can't agree, or if one of you won't admit that there's something wrong, or if someone promises to change but doesn't, you'll find that it's easier to go on to the next step if you've talked about what's going on.

Whatever you fights with friends are about, it's usually helpful to follow some basic ground rules. That way, each person gets to express an opinion but no one is "fighting dirty." Here are a few suggestions:

Stay away from words like *always* and *never*—and avoid insulting words like *stupid, dumb, ugly* and the like. Have you ever heard the expression "fighting words?" Words like *always* and *never* are almost guaranteed to provoke a fight. When someone says, "You *always* forget to call me!" the other person almost *has* to say, "That's not true! What about that time in 1991?" Or "Oh, yeah? Well, *you* never show up on time!" And if someone calls a name like *ugly* or *stupid*, it's almost impossible for the other person to hear anything else that the first person says.

Try to express your own feelings, rather than focusing on what the other person does. "I feel so upset when I'm waiting for you and you don't come" is a lot easier for the other person to hear than, "You're so rude! You just never show up!" It's OK to say, "I'm really angry" or "this makes me really upset." You might even be upset about something that you know the other person can't change. Just stay focused on your feelings, not on the other person's shortcomings.

If the fight is getting really hot, take a few minutes to cool off. This can be hard to do. But if one or the other of you can say, "Time out. Let's take a five-minute break," it can really help the two of you get past the yelling stage and into the working things out period. It also helps if one of you can make a joke—a funny joke about yourself or both of you, not a sarcastic joke at the other person's expense. Saying "Boy, I bet they can hear us in the next county" or "Well, let's get set for Round 2!" might break the worst of the anger with a little laughter.

Try really listening to your friend and then repeating back your friend's points, just the way he or she means them. Then have your friend do the same for you. This way, you can at least be sure that the other person has heard you. You get to avoid exchanges like, "That's not what I meant!" "Well, that's what you said!" "No, it's not!" "Yes, it is—I heard you!" Instead, listen to your friend carefully, and then listen to his or her correction: "No, I 'm not mad that you didn't *go* to Jamie's party. I'm mad that you *said* you were going and then you never showed up!" If you can both finally understand what the other person is saying, you still may not agree—but at least you'll have started communicating.

Don't be afraid to make up. Sometimes two people don't agree for a long time. Sometimes they never agree, but they can still continue to be friends. Decide whether what you and your friend are fighting about is really important to you. If it's important enough to be worth giving up the friendship, so be it. If not, there's no shame in being the one brave enough to make the first move. You might not even have to talk about the fight. Call your friend up and suggest doing something fun together. Or, if you must say something, you might try, "I know we've been fighting, but we can still be friends, can't we?"

When You Stop Being Friends

Sometimes even a good friendship comes to an end. This can be extremely painful, but if you can accept the situation without guilt or shame, that can help to ease the pain.

Why do friendships end? Sometimes two people disagree so deeply about something that they just can't go on being close. Perhaps one friend repeatedly cheats on tests, and the other friend believes this is dishonest. Perhaps one friend enjoys doing drugs or getting drunk, and the second friend believes this is wrong. It may be too hard for the two people to go on hanging out together.

Sometimes friends' interests just grow apart. Perhaps two friends started out enjoying the same games and the same people. Then, as they get older, one friend likes sports while the other prefers fooling around with a computer. Or one friend starts hanging out with a crowd where everybody dates, but the second friend isn't interested in dating yet. These two friends may simply become less close to each other and more close to people with whom they now have more in common.

A sadder case is when one friend drops another because the second friend just "doesn't fit in" with the first friend's new crowd. The two friends may still have a lot in common; they may even enjoy each other's company. But all of a sudden, one friend is "cool," and the other friend is not—and that may be enough to end the friendship.

If you want to keep being friends with someone who is dropping you, ask yourself honestly if it's happening because of anything you did. If possible, talk about it with the friend who's pushing you away. Listen to your friend and look into your own heart to see if there's anything that you can or want to do to change yourself or your behavior. If the answer is no—if there is really nothing you can do—than allow yourself some time to grieve before moving on. Remind yourself that you are a worthwhile person who will have other friends, and do everything you can to spend time with people whom you like and feel comfortable with.

If you are the person who wants to leave the other friend, ask yourself honestly why you're doing it. If you really are no longer interested in being friends, find the least painful way you can of ending the friendship. In some cases, simply being less available will give the other person the message. In other cases, you might want to have a talk with the person or perhaps write him or her a note. You're in a difficult position, but you can make it easier on yourself by being as honest as you can with yourself about what you're doing and why you're doing it. You have a right to pay attention to your own needs and to make your own decisions about who you want to be close to.

Changing Bodies, Changing Relationships

You've been practicing making friends all your life, but it's only recently that you've started thinking about dating. You may not even be interested in dating yet, although you're aware that many of your friends are. Or you may have been interested in dating for a long time. You may be very aware, somewhat aware, or not aware at all of sexual feelings. These feelings may extend to people of the opposite sex, people of your own sex, or both. You might have sexual feelings for people your own age that you really might go out with, or for people who are of a very different age whom you could never really go out with. Or you might have had all of these feelings at different times. It can all be very confusing!

Along with your changing body and changing feelings, you are also dealing with a world that has a wide range of values and standards about sex and relationships. Your family has one set of standards—or perhaps even more than one! Your neighbors may have another; your friends at school may have yet other values. You probably notice that people may have different standards for boys and for girls, for gay relationships and straight ones, for teenagers and adults. Maybe these different standards make sense to you; maybe they just add to the confusion.

It's important to remember that even adults are confused these days about how to conduct sexual relationships. Learning what kinds of behavior feel comfortable to you, how to negotiate with a partner or a date, and how to handle all of the exciting, comforting, scary, and painful feelings that come up in every close relationship is a lifelong job! It may be a job that you're just starting, but remember: Nobody has all the answers! That's why it's important for you to give yourself the time, patience, and support to make sure that you're really doing the things that are right for *you*, no matter what anybody else says or thinks.

Discovering and acting on your own values is one of the hardest things that you will ever do. Gaining the courage, the honesty, and the wisdom to be yourself is part of the journey of becoming an adult. It's a tough journey, but, if you're willing to go the distance, it can be one of the most rewarding things that you will ever do.

What's Right for You?

As you think about the kinds of dating relationships that you want, remember that you are still going through a great many changes. What is right for you today may not be right for you tomorrow. The people you date or want to date are also going through changes as they get older.

A lot of relationship issues are the same as friendship issues. In fact, the suggestions we've made for being a good friend, for fighting and making up in productive ways, and for "breaking up" with friends are pretty much the same for dating relationships as well. Although feelings with people you date may be more intense than your feelings for your friends, the principles of keeping the relationship on a good footing are the same for both.

The major difference, of course, is that with someone you're dating, you may have to negotiate sexual behavior as well as other types of behavior. In this realm in particular, you may feel a great deal of pressure.

Negotiating with Your Partner

If you're a boy, you may feel pressure to "lose your virginity," to prove that you can have sex with a girl; to date or have sex with several girls; or to prove that you're the "boss" in any relationship. These pressures from the outside may not correspond at all to your own feelings. You may not be interested in dating girls at all. Or you may be attracted to girls but not be ready for more than kissing or necking. You may want a more "equal" relationship, where nobody is the "boss," or you may want to be involved with someone who takes the lead emotionally, sexually, or both.

If you're a girl, you may feel under pressure to have sex with your boyfriend or risk losing him. Or you may feel under pressure from your girlfriends, to "catch up" with them as far as sexual experience goes. On the other hand, you may feel pressure—from your friends, your family, or both—to hide or play down your sexual feelings. You may feel uncomfortable admitting how interested you are in sex. You may also have conflicting feelings about who should take the lead or "be the boss" in a sexual relationship.

What's crucial for both boys and girls is to be honest about your own feelings while respecting the feelings of the person you're going out with. If one of you wants to go further than the other one is ready for, that's a problem for the two of you to work out. Perhaps one of you is just ready for more sexual contact at this point in your life. Perhaps the two of you were just born with different sexual needs. Maybe one of you is more attracted than the other, or perhaps one of you needs to feel more secure in the relationship itself before getting physical.

Part of negotiating with a sexual partner is talking about what does and doesn't make you feel good. You may want more cuddling and more affection from your partner, rather than actual sexual contact. Or you may want certain kinds of sexual touching and kissing. Finding a way to communicate this to your partner in an honest and respectful way is part of going out with someone.

Negotiating with someone you're dating is about coming to an agreement that the two of you can both be happy with. It's not an occasion to mock the other person or to put pressure on him or her. Nor is it something for the less ready person to feel guilty about. Nobody owes another person sex, no matter what the circumstance.

A Word About Date Rape

As we have seen, there is room for discussion and negotiation between two people who are dating. What there is not room for is force. No one has the right to force another person into having sex or any kind of sexual contact.

It's important for both boys and girls to understand that a girl always has the right to say "no," at any point, no matter what she has already said "yes" to. A girl might agree to do something sexual and then change her mind. Or she might feel comfortable with kissing a boy but want to say "no" to anything that comes afterward. Either way, girls need to say "no" loud and clear if they mean "no," and boys need to learn to respect that "no."

There are lots of myths that seem to muddy the waters. Some people believe that girls say "no" when they mean "yes." According to this thinking, girls aren't supposed to want sex, so they feel less guilty or less concerned about their reputations if they say "no"—but somehow, boys are able to understand that they really mean "yes."

There may actually be girls who think this way and act this way. Nevertheless, forcing a girl to have sex or sexual contact that she doesn't want is rape, and it's wrong. No matter what a boy *thinks* a girl really means, if she's saying "no," he should pay attention. And girls might need to learn to say, "I mean no, and if you go further, it's rape."

Another myth says that girls use their sexual desirability to tease boys, or that they go ahead and act sexual and then afterward say they didn't mean it. Therefore, a boy that forces sex on a girl is giving her what she really wants—or, at least, what she deserves.

Again, there may be some girls who act like teases. Boys may not want to go out with these girls more than once. They may be hurt or angered by these girls' behavior. That's still no excuse for forcing sex on someone who is saying "no."

Learning More

One of the best things you can do for yourself is to learn more about sex, your own body, and your own responses. There are lots of ways you can do this without committing yourself to a sexual relationship and all its emotional and physical consequences. As you become more interested in sex and relationships, we encourage you to explore these topics on your own, so that you have more choices about the way you handle relationships, and more confidence in your own choices.

One way you can learn more is to read books—both nonfiction and fiction—about sex and relationships. You can share your experiences and insights with friends that you trust. You might even feel comfortable talking with your parents or with other older relatives. Perhaps there is a teacher you trust, or another adult friend. You might also want to explore these topics with a counselor, either a school counselor or a therapist (more on this topic in Chapter 6).

You can gain a sense of physical self-confidence through various kinds of exercise. Playing sports; taking some kind of modern, folk, or ethnic dance class or dancing with friends; jogging; swimming; or other vigorous exercise is a great way to get in touch with your body and to feel good about it from the inside out. The teenage years are often a time when even your own body seems strange, because it is changing so quickly. At times, this may make you feel awkward or clumsy. Committing yourself to some physical activity can help you make friends with your body again, so that you enjoy and savor your own responses.

Gay or Straight?

One common concern among many teenagers is wondering whether they are *homosexual* (having sexual feelings for people of the same sex, gay) or *heterosexual* (having sexual feelings for people of the opposite sex, straight). Because, in many ways, our society has put a stigma on being gay, teenagers may be afraid to find out that they have homosexual feelings. They fear that having these feelings makes them "not real men" or "not real women," and they worry about being teased or worse by their friends, scolded or worse by their family.

In fact, it's common among many teenagers to have strong sexual feelings for people of either sex at some time during their teenage years. Having these feelings doesn't necessarily mean that you intend to act on them. Many teenagers have a range of sexual feelings for both or either sex, then go on as adults to date only people of the opposite sex.

However, many teenagers have strong sexual feelings for people of the same sex that they would like to act on. These teenagers may be bisexual—having sexual feelings for both sexes—or homosexual.

If you think you may be gay or bisexual, you'll have to make your own decisions about how you want to handle these feelings and these choices. Once again, we encourage you to explore your feelings and this subject as fully as possible, so that you get to feel comfortable and empowered making your decisions. Find books to read about gay relationships. See if you can meet gay or bisexual adults through a hot line, a counseling center, or community center. Given our society's stigma on this topic, it may be difficult for you to get support and information but don't give up. You have the right to your feelings and your experiences, and you have the right to support and assistance in making the choices that will work for you.

Sexually Transmitted Diseases (STDs) and Pregnancy

One thing that all teenagers should be aware of is that sexual intercourse is serious business. Besides the emotional involvement that it can create, sex has physical consequences.

One possible consequence of sex between males and females is pregnancy. If you are engaging in sexual intercourse—where the man's penis penetrates the woman's vagina—be sure that you are using birth control. No form of birth control is foolproof, but the most reliable forms are the birth control pill, the diaphragm, the IUD, and the condom used with contraceptive foam. Contraceptive sponges are another possible form of birth control, although they are not as effective as the others. The "rhythm method" (have sex only at certain times of the month) and interrupting sex before the man ejaculates (comes) are *not* reliable methods. They are virtually the same as not using birth control at all; they will almost certainly not protect you from pregnancy.

If you have any questions about birth control, find a clinic or a doctor that will help you get both the information and the contraception that you need. We aren't encouraging anyone to rush into sexual activity. And even with someone you're dating, there are lots of ways to enjoy each other physically without actually having intercourse. But if you do make the decision to have sex, act responsibly. Don't pretend you aren't thinking about it and then get caught without protection.

Another dangerous consequence of sex is sexually transmitted disease (STD). The most well-known and most deadly STD is AIDS—acquired immune deficiency syndrome. When a person is infected with the AIDS virus (HIV), his or her *immune system*—the body's ability to fight off disease—becomes dangerously weakened. The person is then vulnerable to many terrible illnesses, which eventually cause death.

Besides AIDS, a person who is sexually active is vulnerable to several other STDs, including syphilis, gonorrhea, chlamydia, and herpes. There are a variety of ways that these diseases can be transmitted. Generally, if you have any type of sexual intercourse (penis to vagina); oral intercourse (penis to mouth); or anal intercourse (penis to anus, your rear opening), you are risking the transmission of AIDS and other STDs. This is true for both heterosexual and homosexual contact.

The best way to avoid this risk is to avoid this type of sexual contact, restricting yourself to kissing and caressing. The next best form of protection is to use a condom, preferably one with a spermicide. If you have any doubts or questions about how to use this form of protection, find a doctor, a clinic, or a sympathetic adult to show you. It could be a matter of life and death.

Getting the Social Life Your Want

Sometimes it takes a little work to develop the kind of social life you want, particularly if you're looking for the kind of relationships that work best for you, rather than simply going along with your crowd. Each of our composite teenagers had to try some things that didn't work for him or her before arriving at more satisfying relationships.

Unlike most of the guys he knew, Mark didn't think he was very interested in girls. The guys in his crowd were all asking girls out and talking about how far they went with them, so Mark did his best to fit in. He dated a couple of different girls, but no one he really liked, and he never felt like doing any of the things that the other guys talked about.

Mark started to wonder if maybe he was gay. After all, he felt closer to his male friends than to any girl he knew, and he didn't seem to have the sexual feelings for girls that the rest of his crowd did. Then one day one of the biggest talkers in his group let Mark know that most of what he did was just that—talk. Like Mark, he also wasn't very interested in girls, but he hadn't wanted any of the other guys to find out about it.

Mark felt better that he wasn't the only one to feel the way he did, but he still wasn't sure about his own sexuality. Was he really gay, or was he just not yet ready to be interested in girls?

For several weeks, Mark really agonized about this. It seemed to him that being gay would be the worst thing in the world, that he would have an unhappy life and everyone he knew would make fun of him. Having all the guys in his group look down on him seemed too awful even to think about.

Then one day, Mark found out that a famous woman tennis player he'd admired was gay, and so was one of the characters on "Beverly Hills 90210." Neither the real person nor the fictional character seemed to have such an unhappy life, and neither of them seemed to think that there was anything wrong with being gay (although, like Mark, the fictional character was worried about what other people might think).

All of a sudden, Mark felt angry that he'd been so worried. He felt like he'd been letting other people's opinions rule his life. He decided he would try to find out more about being gay by reading about it and by looking for gay organizations in his community. Mark still felt scared about doing something unpopular, but he also wanted to know what his real feelings were. He felt strong thinking that being true to himself was more important to him than worrying about what everyone else thought. Whether or not he was gay, he didn't want his actions to be part of a lie just so he could live up to someone else's image.

Angela enjoyed being on the school paper, but after a while, she decided that what she really wanted was to be in the popular group. It seemed to her that every girl in the popular group had a great boyfriend, and since Angela felt shy about going out with guys, being popular seemed like a solution to her problem.

For a few weeks, Angela tried making friends with one or two girls in the popular group. They seemed to like Angela, and she found herself eating lunch with this new bunch of people. When one of them invited Angela to a party Saturday night, she thought she had it made.

When she actually got to the party, though, Angela was pretty disappointed. Nobody seemed to be talking about anything that was interesting to her; the girls wanted to talk only about clothes, hair, makeup, and boys, and the guys seemed interested only in rating the girls by how they looked. Angela felt really uncomfortable, but she realized that she also felt bored.

Angela decided she was a lot happier with the crowd from the school paper, but she was still shy about how to start dating. As usual, she decided to ask her Aunt Teresa for advice.

Her aunt told her two things that helped a lot. One, Angela should remember that everybody was worried about being rejected and left out, not just her. So she might try being brave enough to do some asking herself. At the very least, she should make it easy for someone else to ask her out by being as friendly and easy-going as she could.

Second, Aunt Teresa suggested that Angela spend as much time as possible in activities where boys and girls did the same kinds of things. Angela was already working on a school paper, which was a good start. If she was looking for another activity, she might think about theater, music, or some kind of coed sports. The less formal the activity, the less likely that boys and girls would be segregated and the more relaxed everyone would be. For example, improvisational theater mixed people together more than theater that followed a written script, where there were separate parts for boys and girls; folk music was more relaxed than singing in a choir divided up among sopranos and basses, and so on.

Slowly, Angela started to follow her aunt's advice. She started saying "hi" to everybody, male or female, and she started as many friendly conversations as she could. Besides her work on the paper, she found time to join the backstage crew of the school drama group, since she had noticed that boys and girls worked together at finding props, making sets, and running lights. She and the crew often went out in a large group, and once or twice, she even managed to ask a guy out for sodas after school. Later, each of those guys asked Angela out to the movies. Since these were guys she had worked with and hung out with in large groups, the dates were a lot more relaxed than Angela had ever imagined they would be. She could tell that, because she was more relaxed, the guys were, too.

Luis was thrilled when he started going out with his girlfriend, Miriam. He felt that she really understood him, and he loved talking to her about the things that were going on in his life. He also felt very attracted to her, and he really enjoyed the physical side of their relationship.

Luis had gone out with a few other girls, plus he had been to a few parties where he had made out with some girls he barely knew. He felt pretty comfortable with a sexual relationship, and he really wanted to express his sexual feelings for Miriam. But Miriam felt differently. She hadn't had as much experience as Luis, and she didn't seem ready to do as much as he wanted.

For a while, Luis thought that if he could just convince Miriam to go along with what he wanted, she would end up liking sex as much as he did. He thought, too, that maybe she was just putting on an act. Maybe Miriam thought she had to *act* like she didn't like heavy petting so that he would still respect her.

Along with his feelings for Miriam, Luis was also very conscious of the other guys he knew. What would they think if they knew that Miriam "called all the shots?" How much would they look down on him if they knew how little she let him do?

Because he thought this way, and because he really liked Miriam, Luis honestly believed that he wasn't doing anything wrong by pressuring her with his words and his actions. Finally, Miriam became very upset. She picked a time at the beginning of a date, before they had gotten to the romantic part of the evening, and told Luis how frustrated and hurt she was that he didn't seem to care what she said or how she felt, that he just went right on arguing with her or going too far physically.

Luis realized that if he wanted to keep seeing Miriam, he had to compromise. His own sexual feelings were very strong, and he was also pretty worried about what his friends would say, so he did think about breaking up with her. Finally, though, he decided that he'd rather compromise than miss being with Miriam altogether. He also discovered that when he stopped pushing so hard, Miriam had more space to enjoy herself and was actually more responsive.

Luis also decided to tell Miriam how he felt, without pushing or teasing. When he did, he saw that she now respected *his* feelings, even if she couldn't go along with them completely.

Luis still feels like he is compromising to some extent. But he and Miriam are both much happier now that they're really communicating.

Developing the social life you want and creating the relationships that work for you can be a lifelong process, one that grows and changes as you grow and change, too. If you can stay in touch with your own feelings while learning to negotiate with a partner, if you can balance your desire for independence with your wish to be accepted by your friends, you will have learned a valuable lesson that will stay with you for the rest of your life. And, along the way, you'll enjoy a social life that works for you because it fits who you really are.

5

School Problems,
Home Problems

As you struggle to make good choices about schoolwork, extracurricular activities, and your social life, you may feel frustrated, worried, or angry about problems at school or at home that get in your way. These problems may not be of your making, but nevertheless, you've got to deal with them. If they are serious enough, they can take up so much of your time, emotions, and energy that you have very little left for studying or socializing.

If something is really upsetting you, to the point where you can't concentrate on your studying or enjoy some time with your friends, we urge you to deal with it right away. If you need to, get support and help, so that you don't have to deal with the problem by yourself.

Some people deal with their problems by picking fights, acting "down," or doing poorly in school. They may be hoping that if they are miserable or angry enough, if they have problems so big and dramatic that no one could miss them, then someone will notice their real problem and help them out. In fact, if this is what you're doing, it's more likely that people won't recognize the reasons for it. Instead, they'll simply get mad at you or leave you alone, which will only make you feel worse. If you are having trouble with something, do your best to identify the problem and to do something about it. That way, you've got a fighting chance to solve the problem.

In Chapter 6, we talk about various ways of getting help; in Chapter 7, we list some kinds of help that might be available. In this chapter, we'll identify some common problems at school and at home. If any of them ring a bell for you, muster your courage and do something to make life easier for yourself. It's no more than you deserve!

Before we get on to the problems, though, here's one all-purpose solution that you might try. Try to find at least one adult at your school whom you really like. It might be a teacher or a counselor—but it might also be a janitor, a secretary, or the cashier in the school cafeteria. Just knowing someone who cares whether you had a hard test or a bad fight with your folks—or a great date or a winning basketball game—will make both your school and your world seem like a friendlier place. And an adult may have ideas, resources, or influence that will really help you when you're facing a problem that's too big for you to handle alone.

Problems that Might Come up at School

Gangs and Violence

Some schools have groups that go beyond cliques—they have gangs. If your school is one of these, you've got a difficult problem indeed to face. You'll have to be very clever and thoughtful about finding ways to survive and even to thrive under these circumstances.

If your school is full of gangs, or if it is a violent place in other ways, you might look into the possibility of transferring to another school. This is tricky, but it can be done. (See the next chapter for some suggestions on how to look into this.) You might also look for older students whom you admire or students who have graduated and ask them about their strategies for survival. If you are not in a gang, you will have to decide if it works best for you to avoid the people who are perpetrating the violence, or if there is some way in which you need to confront them in order to make sure they leave you alone. Whatever you decide, let your decision be guided by what's going to be best for you, now and in the future, as you follow your own dreams about the kind of life you want. That may serve you better than being guided by your temper, your resentment, or by a need to show other people that you aren't afraid.

Some students who aren't in gangs think about carrying weapons to protect themselves. Again, this is a decision only you can make, so it's a choice you'll need to think through very carefully. This might seem like an effective way to protect yourself. But you may be taking the risk of getting arrested, even going to jail, for doing something illegal. Of course, you're also risking the possibility of killing another person, either accidentally or on purpose. How do these possibilities fit in with the kind of person you want to become and the kind of future you want to have?

If you're already in a gang, then you already know how tough it is to get out. Usually, a guy can get out of a gang easily only by becoming a father—and that may seem like too high a price for you to pay. If you leave your gang under any other circumstances, you risk getting harassed, even badly beaten up. And you have to be willing to be a loner, since gang members and non-gang members alike will probably go out of their way to avoid a former gang member. Still, if you are determined to leave your gang, you might be willing to pay these prices. After all, consider the price of staying in your gang, the risks of death and danger to yourself and to your family.

Sometimes transferring to another school will help you to leave a gang, although your reputation may follow you from school to school. You might be able to find someone else who left a gang and find out how he managed it. The important thing is to keep remembering that there is *always* a choice, even if it's a difficult or unpleasant one, even if it takes a lot of work to find it.

If you are in a violent school situation, you might see if there is some way that your community can respond to this problem. Perhaps there is already a parents' group or a community group that is organized to do something about violence in your neighborhood. Perhaps you and other concerned students could help start such a group, either at school or in your community. Frequently problems that an individual can't solve alone can be solved when people get together.

Budget Cuts and Underfunded Schools

Recently published books have shown that there is an enormous gap between the best-funded and the worst-funded schools in the United States. That's because public schools are funded through a combination of local property taxes and state and federal funds. Wealthier neighborhoods have more expensive property and higher taxes; hence, there is more money for the schools there. Under the severe budget cuts of the 1980s and early 1990s, even less money has been available to the poorer schools. Although all children are supposed to have an equal opportunity at a public education, the shameful fact is that some schools really cannot afford to offer as much opportunity as others.

If this is the situation at your school, you may be feeling the effects of your school's lack of funding in a very personal way. Perhaps there are not enough textbooks or your textbooks are out of date. Maybe you don't have enough lab equipment, art supplies, or sports equipment; maybe there is no budget to have a school orchestra or sponsor a school play. You may be going to school in a deteriorating building, with broken windows, a leaky roof, inadequate heat or ventilation. Maybe your classes have so many students that the teachers cannot provide you with the individual attention you need.

Inequality in public education is one of the most unfair situations of our time. You shouldn't have to put up with it. But if you do, you might consider what you can do about it.

Part of what's demoralizing about going to an underfunded school is that it can give you the message that you aren't important—you just don't rate a good school with working equipment. So the first thing to remember is that you are important. "Society" may be giving you a negative message, but you don't have to believe it. It may take work to push that message away and replace it with a more positive message, but which type of person would you rather be: one who gives in to the people who are trying to tear you down, or someone who fights back and succeeds in getting what you want?

Once again, if you're attending an underfunded school, you might consider the possibility of transferring to a better place. (See the next chapter for suggestions.) It's difficult, but sometimes it can be done. If you can't or don't want to do that, think about ways in which you can find resources to supplement what's missing at your school. Is there a public library that has a better selection than your school library? Do community centers or neighborhood organizations have their own libraries or collections of material? Are there adults in your neighborhood who can be your resources, who can help you study, who can come to your school and speak about what they know? Perhaps there's a local college or community college whose students and professors might be resources, as tutors, guest speakers, leaders of field trips, or in some other way. Can local radio, television, and newspaper journalists share their knowledge and their libraries with you? What about neighborhood doctors and lawyers? What other adults in your community have something to offer to help make up for the lack of funding at your school?

Once again, you might want to consider the possibilities of getting together with other students, or possibly also with teachers and parents, to help enrich your school. You may feel that the problems around you are too big for you to take on, but you don't have to take them on alone. Look around for other people who feel the way you do and see if together you can come up with creative responses. You may be surprised by how empowering it is to organize for change.

Problems that Can Come up at Home

Sometimes the problems you are facing at home are so severe that they can interfere with your ability to think about anything else. If that's the case, we urge you to do something about them. There's no point in sitting at your desk, trying to force your brain to focus, when you've got something more important preying on your mind.

Once you've taken the first step toward solving your other problems, we suggest that you do what you can to at least maintain your schoolwork. Perhaps you can tell your teachers what is going on, or get a counselor, teacher, or other adult to speak to your teachers for you. Together, you may be able to work out a plan that will at least keep you from failing. Maybe you can figure out a bare minimum of work to lay the foundation for making improvements later.

When You Have a Problem with Drugs or Alcohol

You may find that your involvement with drugs or alcohol is having a big effect on your life. Maybe you feel strung out or hung over a lot of the time. Perhaps you're constantly worried about how to get the liquor or drugs that you feel you need to make it through the day or the week. You may find that getting high is interfering with your ability to concentrate on your schoolwork, in class or at home.

If your life is organized around drinking or drugs, or if you think that your schoolwork or other parts of your life may be suffering, you might try this experiment: Give up drinking and drugs completely for 30 days. See what happens. See how you feel. If you find yourself feeling anxious, desperate, or depressed—or if just the thought of 30 "straight" days brings on that feeling—then you have a problem. The activity that you started "just for fun" is now bringing you more misery than pleasure. See the next two chapters for ways that you can get help.

When a Friend or Relative Has a Drug or Alcohol Problem

Someone else's drug or alcohol problem can be even harder to deal with than a problem of your own. One of the most painful things about someone else's addiction is realizing that you can't change the other person's behavior. That's a decision that the other person has to make alone.

What you can do, however, is make your own decision to get the help you need. If one or both of your parents has a drug or alcohol problem, your situation is especially urgent. The substance abuse may be connected to other types of abuse, such as physical violence, physical neglect, or sexual abuse. (For more about these problems, read on.) Or you may simply be living in an unstable atmosphere, where you never know when a fight will break out or some other crisis will emerge. Perhaps your brothers and sisters or one of your parents expects you to take on extra work and responsibility to compensate for the addicted person. Perhaps you feel, deep down, that the other person's problem is somehow your fault; or maybe you feel guilty for being so angry at this person you're supposed to love.

If a family member, especially a parent, has a drug or alcohol problem, life has dealt you an unfair situation—but there is something you can do about it. Look in the next two chapters to find out more about getting help. Then call a hot line, contact Al-Anon (a group for the friends and families of alcoholics), Al-A-Teen (a branch of Al-Anon especially for teenagers), a social service agency, or a counselor. Don't let someone else's problem ruin you life.

Physical and Sexual Abuse

It's your parents' job to provide you with a safe and nurturing environment. Sometimes you may feel that they're not doing a very good job. But you know that conflicts between parents and teenagers are part of the normal give and take of family life and that sometimes all you can do is grin and bear it. How can you tell when you're dealing with conflict or difficulties that you should *not* have to put up with?

It's your right not to have to deal with physical or sexual abuse. Physical abuse—also known as child abuse—is any kind of physical contact that causes pain or injury, including slapping, punching, kicking, burning, throwing things at someone, and beatings with a belt or strap. Physical abuse is any kind of physical contact that leaves a scar, a welt, a burn, or another type of injury. If this kind of activity is going on in your house, directed at you or at someone else, get help. Physical abuse is against the law, and you should not have to put up with it.

Sexual abuse is any kind of sexual contact between a parent and child, between siblings (brothers and sisters), between an older teenager and a young child, or between an adult and a teenager. It can include vaginal, oral, or anal intercourse, petting and caressing, tickling, and kissing. It can also include being watched while getting dressed or using the bathroom, or being made to watch while someone else does; listening to someone talk in a "dirty" or sexually explicit way or being asked to talk "dirty" or explicitly yourself. Sexual abuse can happen with adults of either sex and with children of either sex, in any combination, male-female, female-male, male-male, or female-female. An adult who has no other gay relationships may sexually abuse a child of the same sex.

Sometimes children enjoy some parts of the contact in sexual abuse. They may like being hugged—but not want the hug to be a sexual one. They may enjoy the love and attention they are getting—but feel uncomfortable about the sexual nature of the contact. Just because a child enjoys some parts of sexual abuse does not make him or her responsible for the abuse. No matter what the child has done, the adult is always responsible for sexual abuse.

Your body and your feelings belong to you, and you have the right to be free of any unwanted sexual contact. If you are being sexually or physically abused, tell someone about it. Tell a friend, a sympathetic adult, an anonymous hot line, a counselor, or a social service agency. If you tell someone who doesn't believe you, find someone else to tell, and don't give up until you get the help you deserve. (For more about getting help, see the next two chapters.)

Emotional Abuse, Divorce, and Other Troubles at Home

Physical and sexual abuse are against the law, and problems with drugs or alcohol are pretty clear-cut. But sometimes the problems at home don't fit into such straightforward categories. What if your parents simply fight all the time, and it's getting you down? What if they're always picking on you, so that you're starting to feel that you can't do anything right? What if they're always saying how much they love you, but they never want to hug you or spend any time with you? What if they seem depressed or upset when you report a triumph or a good day, and seem comforting and loving only when you've had a problem or a setback?

One of the painful parts of becoming a teenager is realizing that your parents are only human, with weaknesses, fears, and failures that are bound to affect you and your life. Even the best parents in the world are only human—and some parents are very far from being the best.

The pain of watching your parents go through their own problems may be even more severe if they are in the process of getting a divorce, and particularly if they themselves are dating or starting new relationships. The teenage years are *your* turn to try out dating and relationships; you may feel frightened, angry, or jealous that your parents are doing what you feel you're supposed to be doing.

It's never easy to deal with the shortcomings of parents, because we all grew up needing our parents to help keep us alive. As children, we had to believe that these big people could do anything in the world, since we needed their strength for our protection.

Now that you're older, you're more able to take care of yourself, so you're more willing and able to see what your parents cannot do. They may not always be able to give you what you need—or even what you have a right to expect from parents. This is painful and unfair, but if it is your situation, you will need to find a way to deal with it. Are there other adults whom you can turn to: a relative, a teacher, the parent of a friend? Would it help you to get counseling or to join a support group?

You might also go into yourself to find your own resources and defenses. If your parents are constantly criticizing, insulting, or undermining you, you might try talking with them and explaining how their behavior makes you feel. If that doesn't work, you might work on ways of avoiding contact with your parents. When you have to be in touch with them, you might picture a magic shield or force field that surrounds you, protecting you from the insults or criticisms that they throw at you. This won't get you the emotional support that you do need, but at least it will minimize the effects of the abuse.

Thoughts of Suicide

If your problems are getting you down so far that death seems like the only way out, you need to take action *now*. Find someone to tell your thoughts and feelings to: a hot line, a friend, a sympathetic adult, or a counselor. Even if you feel that others have let you down in the past—or that you have let yourself down—don't give up now. Help is out there, and you can find it.

You Are Not Alone

Sometimes the worst thing about having a problem is feeling like you're the only one in the world who has it. The isolation and the sense of shame can be almost worst than the problem itself.

Each of our composite teenagers had to face that type of isolation, either in themselves or in people they knew. As you read about the problems they faced, can you imagine the solutions they might find?

Mark has always enjoyed hanging out and partying with his friends. His best friend, Pete, whom he studies with, likes to party, too. In fact, Mark is starting to get worried about Pete. Lately it seems like Pete is always either high or hung over. Pete has always been such a good student that Mark was getting help from him, but now Pete is frequently late with assignments and doesn't seem to do so well on tests. When Mark asks him about it, Pete just brushes the whole problem away. The other day, Mark thought he saw Pete sleeping in class behind the dark glasses he was wearing. He also thought he smelled liquor on Pete at school, although he can't quite believe that Pete is drinking during the day. In any case, Mark is afraid to tell Pete that he might be drinking too much. What if Pete gets mad or acts really insulted? Or even worse, what if he turns on Mark and starts telling Mark about all the things that are wrong with *him?*

For a while, Angela has been frustrated with how her parents have been treating her. She's always had a lot more housework and responsibilities at home than other kids her age. Recently, though, her mother got laid off, and instead of going back out and looking for another job, she just seemed to collapse. She gets terrible migraines and dizzy spells and has to spend a lot of time in bed. Everyone in the family expects that Angela will give up all her after-school activities in order to come home and take up the slack. Even when Angela's mother isn't actually sick, she still acts in a strange way. Sometimes she talks baby talk to Angela, as though she is the little girl and Angela is the mother. Even though she does this in a joking way, it upsets Angela. When Angela mentions this to her father, he gets furious with her, as though she is the one causing all the problems. He tells her that if she would just do her chores, her mother wouldn't have so much to worry about, and then maybe she'd get better.

Luis has been trying very hard to make things work for him at school, but sometimes it just gets to be too much. Last year they cut the school baseball team. This year, the school is short on textbooks, so in some classes, the kids actually have to share. Luis has heard how important computers are in today's job market, and he'd really like to learn how to use one, but his school is too poor to afford even one cheap computer. Luis's cousin goes to school across town, in a more expensive neighborhood, and Luis knows that the kids in that other school are learning all the latest programs on all the latest models. Not having enough opportunities at school makes Luis feel really angry, as though someone is telling him that he's just not worth paying attention to. It also makes him feel really discouraged, as though he's doomed to never getting an interesting, high-paying job or ever having the kind of life he wants.

There are many different things that Mark, Angela, and Luis can do to respond to their problems. What advice would you give them? Think of your own solutions, and then read on to see whether Chapter 6 gives you even more ideas.

6

Getting Help

People need help with all sorts of problems in life. Sometimes they need practical help: to be taught a skill, given directions, or supplied with information. Sometimes they need emotional help: to be comforted in times of grief, to find clarity in times of confusion. As you look at your life at school, you may find that you need help with schoolwork, with extracurricular activities, with your social life, or with some aspect of your personal or family life that is interfering with your ability to get the most out of school. This chapter is about identifying and getting the kind of help you need. Chapter 7 offers some specific suggestions of places and resources that might help you.

Sometimes, when you need help most, it's particularly difficult to ask for it. Perhaps you feel ashamed of needing help, believing that you should be able to solve your problems on your own. Perhaps you're discouraged about the possibility that anyone else could help you. Your parents or other important people may have let you down in the past, so you find it hard to believe that anyone else could do any better. Perhaps you feel guilty about asking for help, because it means exposing a secret or a problem concerning your family or a friend, or because you believe that your problems spring from a bad thing that you did.

These are all common feelings that many people share. If these feelings are keeping you from getting the help you need, perhaps you can find a way to acknowledge these feelings—and also to get in touch with other feelings that you may have. Is there a part of you, however small, that believes in a better life than the one you've got right now? Is there a voice inside you, however soft, that is saying "You can do it!" or "You deserve good things, too!" Find and nurture those parts of you, and draw on their strength as you think about getting the help you need.

Places to Look for Help

- Your guidance counselor or principal's office
- A sympathetic teacher, relative, or other adult
- Another student who has had the same problem
- Your parents (You might be surprised at how helpful they can be once they know what's wrong!) or an older brother or sister
- The first few pages of the telephone directory, or the section that includes government agencies
- Advertisements in public places (government agencies often have billboards or other advertisements)
- Chapter 7 of this book

Ways to Ask for Help—From Anybody

- Be honest. If you don't say clearly what the problem is, how can anyone figure out how to help you?

- Don't give up. If you believe someone hasn't understood what you've said, find another way to say it. If you believe the person you're talking to can't or won't understand you, find another person to talk to.
- Be willing to listen. Perhaps the person you're talking to does understand you—but is giving you information that you'd rather not hear. You may have hoped that the person will reassure you that a problem isn't really so bad, when in fact, it's very serious. It's hard, but see if you can separate your emotional reactions from your judgment about what the person is saying.
- Always leave with a concrete plan for what you'll do next, even if it's only to set up another meeting with the person. Then, if you start feeling bad about your problem again, you can remind yourself that you have a plan.
- Take it one day at a time. Your problem probably didn't spring up overnight, so it isn't going to go away overnight. If you imagine yourself still enduring this problem 10 years from now, of course you're going to be discouraged. Just concentrate on getting through today, and let tomorrow take care of itself.
- Be good to yourself. You may have made some mistakes—everybody has. You may still be making mistakes—everybody does. The important thing is not to avoid every single mistake, but to keep working toward being the kind of person you want to be and having the kind of life you want to have. Keep focused on that goal, and forgive yourself for your part in your problems.

Getting Help from Your Parents

Maybe you're having trouble with schoolwork. You might be having a conflict with a teacher, or you might believe that your school is treating you unfairly, perhaps because of your race or sex. Or maybe your problems have their source at home, in conflicts with parents or other family members.

If you decide to talk with your parents, pick a quiet, relaxed time to do it. Let your parents know that you've got something important to talk about and ask them to make a time to sit down in calm and privacy to discuss it. Make sure you convey how seriously you're taking this discussion, so they can take it seriously too.

Find a way to express the problem without blame. Just stay focused on your own feelings and your own situation. If your problem concerns schoolwork, be honest about how serious you think the situation is. If your problem has something to do with a mistake you made—cheating on a test, breaking some school rule—be honest about what you've done. You may have been living with your problem for a long time, but this may be the first your parents have heard of it, so be prepared for them to need some time to adjust to what you're telling them. Their reactions may be upsetting, painful, or scary to you, but stay focused on your goal: expressing what's going on and getting help.

Getting Help from a Teacher

If you decide to take this route, pick the teacher or administrator you feel most comfortable with, and start by talking to him or her. If you don't know whom to talk to, ask around. Maybe one of your friends or another student will have had a good experience with someone whom you can also talk to.

When you've chosen a person, let him or her know that you want to have a talk and ask when would be a good time. If you drop into a teacher's classroom just as she is getting ready to go home, she may not have time for you right then—and she may not realize that you have a serious problem to talk about. If you are going to ask someone for help, give the person a chance to really help you by letting them know what you need.

Once you've set up time to talk, again, be honest. If you want to make sure that your parents don't hear about the talk, or that it stays confidential, say so at the beginning of the conversation and get the person's agreement to respect your wishes. You should know, however, that teachers and school personnel are bound by law to report physical and sexual abuse. Talking to a school employee may set a chain of events in motion whether you want it to or not. We believe that it's always better to tell someone about abuse, that the consequences are always better than letting the abuse continue. But it's your decision.

Be as complete as possible when you're talking about the problem. If it's a home problem, give examples. If it's a school problem, see if you can identify how long it's been going on, what classes it affects, and any other details that will help the teacher figure out what's likely to be going on.

Once again, if you don't get the help you need from the first person you tell, don't give up. Find someone else. If no one in your school is willing to find you a tutor, find your own. Go to the local college, post an ad in a library or at a community center, ask around among older students or honors classes. If you can't afford to pay in money, work out a labor exchange. It's your education. Be creative and be committed!

Getting Help from a Counselor

Whether you talk to a counselor inside or outside of school, you have the right to expect privacy and confidentiality. If these are concerns of yours, go over the ground rules with the counselor first, before you talk about your problem. Be aware, though, that they too are bound by law to report physical or sexual abuse so that the abuse can stop.

When you first go to a counselor, you may feel that all you want is just to talk. It may feel like an enormous relief just to tell someone else about the problem you've been carrying around by yourself. You may find that just talking makes you feel better or gives you some ideas.

You may also find that talking about your problem brings up the pain, grief, anger, or fear that you have been trying to avoid. A good counselor can help you handle these feelings as they come up. Though this process can be difficult, the rewards are well worth it. Once you're not stuffing your feelings away, you have a chance to deal with the real issues. And you may be amazed at how much lighter you feel without all those buried feelings!

After you've gone over the reason you need help, it's often useful to talk to the counselor about all the ground rules. Find out what kind of help the person can offer, and what he or she expects from you in return. The counselor may want you to commit to regular appointments, to showing up on time for appointments, or to other kinds of scheduling. He or she may make suggestions for you to try between sessions or may suggest other resources for you, such as a support group. Make sure you and your counselor have the same idea about what each of you expects from the other.

If you don't believe that a counselor is really understanding you or is really on your side, you may want to find another counselor. Of course, every counselor may have occasion to tell you something you don't want to hear or that you find difficult to accept, but if you have a basic sense of trust in the person, you can work through those times. Be willing to give your counselor an honest chance—but pay attention to your instincts, too.

When You Want to Change Schools

The rules for transferring to another school vary from place to place. However, if you understand the basic principles involved, you'll be better able to negotiate a change in schools, if that's what you decide you want.

Public schools in the United States are organized on the basis of school districts. A school district is a geographical area whose property taxes all go into the same budget to pay for the schools in that area. Within a district, there is likely to be at least one elementary school, one middle school or junior high, and one high school. Usually, in every district, there are several smaller elementary schools for every large high school. That's because elementary schools are generally made up of single classrooms where students learn everything from one teacher (perhaps with some support from a visiting art or music teacher), whereas high schools offer specialized courses that not every student wants to take. Therefore, it's more efficient to have more students at a high school, so that specialized courses can be filled.

What this means for you is that the higher up you go, the fewer schools you'll have to choose from within your district. Generally, it's much easier to transfer within a school district than outside of it. That's because if you stay within a school district, your parents' taxes still go to support the school you're attending. If you transfer out of your district, you're attending a school paid for by somebody else's parents. School officials are usually reluctant to take in outside students for fear that their taxpayer base will be angry about supporting education for "outsiders."

So the first thing for you to find out about is what the options are within your district. You still will need special permission to attend a different school than the one assigned to you, but your district officials will have a lot more latitude than the officials of another district.

Since school districts are funded by property taxes, schools in poor neighborhoods have smaller budgets than schools in the more expensive areas. You may feel frustrated in looking at the options within your district, and then noting that the students across town and in another district are enjoying a far better selection of classes and a much wider range of extracurricular programs—and of course, this situation is unfair to you. However, there may also be a wide range of school quality within a single district, so it's to your advantage to check these out first.

The next thing to do is to find out what your district's rules are for transferring. A sympathetic teacher or counselor may be able to tell you. If you feel alienated from the teachers and officials at your school, you might try finding a savvy adult to help you—perhaps even another school employee, such as a cashier or janitor. If you have your parents' support, they can also make some phone calls to your school district to find out the rules and procedures. You might also make these calls yourself; check the blue pages in the phone directory or ask directory assistance for the name of your school district.

You will probably find that a student needs to have a concrete reason for transferring. Just getting along badly with most of the teachers or feeling turned off by the violent atmosphere of a school will probably not be considered a good reason. Officials tend to think that if they let one student transfer for these reasons, they would have to let many more do so, too. And then what would they do about those schools that nobody wants to go to?

However, if you can demonstrate a need or interest in a particular course offered elsewhere, or in an extracurricular activity, you are likely to have a much better case for transferring. What you'll need to do, with or without the help of an adult, is psych out the mentality of the people who make the decisions on transferring in your district. Find out what they consider good reasons or a good case, and then do everything you can to present your situation accordingly. You're likely to get much further with your parents' full support, or at least with some adult who can speak for you; rightly or wrongly, officials tend not to take student complaints very seriously, but they feel more obliged to listen to taxpayers.

The same goes for transferring outside your district. It may be tricky, but it can be done—especially if you have the support of a teacher, a guidance counselor, or someone from inside the system who can be your advocate. A community group, a politician, or a neighborhood activist can also be a valuable ally. If getting a good education is worth a bit of a struggle to you, and if you believe that transferring is the way to do it, then start your research process now. You may eventually have to take no for an answer, but you just might work out a better deal for yourself.

Moving On

What about our three composite teenagers? How did they go about finding the help they needed?

Mark finally decided that he had to say something to Pete about Pete's drinking problem. He picked a time when he and Pete were alone, hanging out after a fairly pleasant study session. Mark had really thought a lot about how to express his point of view. He gave concrete examples of what he saw Pete doing that concerned him—the sleeping in class, the falling grades—and he stayed focused on his own feelings about what he saw. ("I see this stuff going on, and it scares me for you. I'm really worried about you getting in an accident, or just messing up your future.")

Nevertheless, Pete hit the ceiling. His reaction was even worse than Mark had feared. At first, he tried to make a joke out of it, but when Mark wouldn't back down, he started yelling that what he did was none of Mark's business and that Mark wasn't so perfect either. He started listing all of Mark's problems to show how Mark had no grounds for saying anything to Pete.

Mark felt terrible about Pete's reaction. He worried that he had lost his best friend, and he also worried that maybe Pete was right, maybe he was just using Pete's problems to make himself feel superior.

Then, about three weeks later, Pete got into a slight accident driving while drunk. He wasn't hurt too badly, but he realized that he could have been killed—and he could have killed somebody else. He came back to Mark and agreed that maybe he had a problem, but he was scared and he didn't know how to handle it. He told Mark that since the accident, he'd been trying to cut back on his drinking, but he just wasn't able to. It scared him being so out of control.

Together, Mark and Pete tried to figure out what to do. Mark remembered that on the television show "Beverly Hills 90210," one of the coolest characters also had a drinking problem and went to meetings of Alcoholics Anonymous. He also remembered that he'd seen notices about A.A. meetings at his church. He offered to go with Pete to a meeting, and Pete agreed.

Mark was very relieved that his friend was going to get help. But he knew that if Pete had not had the accident, he might have stayed mad at Mark. Mark realized that he had cared enough about Pete to risk losing his friendship.

Angela had a very hard time even admitting she had a problem. Deep down inside, she kind of agreed with her father: She believed that if she could just be a better daughter, her mother would not be in such bad shape. So she felt ashamed of being such a bad daughter, and she didn't want to admit her shame to anybody else, or even to herself.

Angela also felt very angry with her mother for acting like such a baby. But then she felt guilty about feeling angry. And in some ways, it was easier to be mad at herself than to be mad at her mother, because Angela also really loved her mother and wanted her to get well. It scared Angela to see her mother acting helpless, especially since it seemed to scare her father, too.

Finally, Angela felt guilty about telling anybody outside the family that her mother had a problem. It seemed like betraying her mother. She felt more strongly this way when even Aunt Teresa refused to help her. Her aunt told her that family problems should stay inside the family, and that Angela should just grin and bear it.

Angela's mixed-up feelings of anger, guilt, fear, and love kept preying on her mind. Although she had been getting better organized, now she found herself feeling scattered and anxious again. Her teachers noticed that she was distracted in class, and her friends thought she seemed down. But Angela managed to keep her grades up, and she was such a naturally cheerful person that no one really suspected that anything serious was wrong.

Finally, Angela decided she just couldn't take it any more. She went to see the school counselor, who agreed to keep all conversations private. Since Angela wasn't actually being abused or badly treated, the counselor had no obligation to talk to Angela's family. But Angela noticed an enormous feeling of relief as she talked to someone about her problem. The counselor helped her understand that she could have all of her different emotions without feeling guilty, and she also helped Angela realize that her mother's problems were not Angela's fault. Things are still difficult at home for Angela, but now she feels that she has someone in her corner.

Luis kept on being angry about how little money was available at his school. Even though he had become very resourceful—like when he found another baseball team after his school team was cut—he still resented that he had to go to so much trouble when the kids across town had better schools and better programs without doing anything about it.

Finally, Luis decided that he wanted to take some kind of action to make things better. Maybe he couldn't fix everything right away, but he knew he'd rather be doing something than just complaining or feeling discouraged.

It took Luis a while to figure out how to take action in a way that would work. At first, he circulated a petition among the other kids at school, thinking that for sure everyone would sign. But to his surprise, most kids felt so discouraged that they wouldn't even put their names on a piece of paper.

What did come out of the petition drive, though, was four or five other students who felt the way Luis did. They started meeting together to figure out how they could make things better at their school. Finally, they decided to go to the meeting of a local community group, in order to ask the group to help them fight for more school funding.

Their first meeting was a disaster. Luis hadn't told anyone they were coming, so the students had to sit through a whole meeting that didn't seem to have anything to do with them. At the end of the meeting, someone finally asked why they were there. Even though the meeting was almost over, a couple of regular members volunteered to meet with the high school students another time. Now they're on their third meeting, coming up with all sorts of plans: a march on the city council, a citywide petition drive, or a meeting with the school superintendent. Luis thinks that once they've chosen a concrete plan, he and the other students might be able to get still more students to take part. Even though he knows it's a slow process, he feels excited to be a part of a group that's making change happen.

Education for Your Life

Throughout this book, we've talked about a wide range of topics: schoolwork, extracurricular activities, social life, home and school problems, and getting help. Every student will have his or her own style in dealing with these areas; every reader of this book will have his or her own opinions about what works best. But every reader should also take away the same message: Don't give up. Figure out the kind of school experience that's right for you, the kind of future that you want to have, the kind of person you want to be—and then do everything in your power to make it happen. Learning what you want and how to go after it may be the most important thing you can learn from your time in school.

7

Where to Find Help

The following organizations will be able to provide you with referrals and advice in dealing with a variety of problems or crises that you may have to deal with.

Alcohol and Drug Problems

Al-Anon Family Group
  Headquarters
1372 Broadway
New York, NY 10036
212-302-7240
See the white pages for the group in your area. Al-Anon helps those over the age of 13 deal with alcohol problems in their families.

Alcoholics Anonymous and
  World Services
468 Park Avenue South
New York, NY 10016
212-870-3400
This organization provides free referrals for those seeking recovery from alcohol problems.

ALCOHOL Helpline
1-800-944-4769
This organization provides counseling and referrals to treatment centers or self-help groups.

Narcotics Anonymous World
  Services Office
16155 Wyandotte Street
Van Nuys, CA 91406
818-780-3951
This organization provides general reference services for those seeking recovery from narcotics addiction.

National Cocaine Hotline
1-800-262-2463
This service helps cocaine users, their friends and families.

Pills Anonymous
130 West 72nd Street
New York, NY 10023
212-874-0700
This group offers support for people with drug dependency problems.

Birth Control and Family Planning

American College of Obstetrics and Gynecology
1-800-762-2264
This service provides free brochures on birth control.

Those in the following states can call for additional advice, for information.

New Jersey: 1-800-624-2637
Illinois: 1-800-843-3228
Tennessee: 1-800-255-4936
West Virginia: 1-800-642-8522

Planned Parenthood Federation of America
810 Seventh Avenue
New York, NY 10019
212-541-7800
This organization provides information on birth control and sexuality.

National Abortion Federation Hotline
1-800-772-9100
This hot line tells where to get a safe abortion.

Civil Liberties and Human Rights

The following organizations provide information, referrals, and, in some cases, legal assistance in all areas of discrimination.

American Civil Liberties Union (ACLU)
132 West 43rd Street
New York, NY 10036
212-944-9800

Children's Legal Rights Information and Training Program
2008 Hillyer Place
Washington, DC 20009
202-332-6575

Civil Rights Division
Department of Justice
Room 5643
10th Street and Constitution Avenue NW
Washington, DC 20530
202-633-2151

International League for Human Rights
432 Park Avenue South
New York, NY 10016
212-684-1221

Eating Disorders

National Association of Anorexia Nervosa and Associated Disorders, Inc. (ANAD)
P.O. Box 7
Highland Park, IL 60035
312-831-3438

National Eating Disorders Information Center
200 Elizabeth Street
C-W 1-328
Toronto, Ontario
Canada 2C4 M5G
416-340-4156

Emotional Problems

National Institutes of Mental
  Health
301-443-4513
This organization provides referrals for psychological counseling.

The Handicapped/
Physically Challenged

These organizations provide resources for the disabled:

American Council of the Blind
1-800-424-8666

National Association of the Deaf
301-587-1788

National Information Center for
  Handicapped Children and
  Youth with Disabilities
P.O. Box 1492
Washington, DC 20013
703-893-6061

National Organization on Disability
  (NOD)
1-800-248-2253

Office of Special Education and
  Rehabilitative Services
Clearinghouse on the Handicapped
Dept. of Education
Switzer Building, Room 3132
330 C Street SW
Washington, DC 20202
202-732-1241

Washington Connection
1-800-424-8666
Gives recorded information about
legislation affecting the blind.

Physical and Sexual Abuse

American Humane Association
63 Inverness Drive East
Englewood, CO 80112
303-792-9900
This group protects children
against neglect and abuse.

Big Brothers–Big Sisters of America
230 North 13th Street
Philadelphia, PA 19107
215-567-7000
This group helps children and teens,
including matching children from
single-family homes with adults.

Boys Town, U.S.A.
Communications and Public
  Service Division
14100 Crawford Rd.
Boys Town, NE 68010
402-498-1111 (office)
1-800-448-3000 (national hot line)

Child Abuse Listening Mediation,
  Inc. (CALM)
P.O. Box 90754
Santa Barbara, CA 93190-0754
805-569-2255
Combats child abuse through family
therapy and community education.

Childhelp/International
6463 Independence Avenue
Woodland Hills, CA 91370
1-800-4-A-CHILD
Childhelp provides crisis counseling, information, and referrals in situations dealing with child abuse.

Clearinghouse on Child Abuse
  and Neglect Information
(a division of the National Center
on Child Abuse and Neglect/

Children's Bureau-NCCAN)
P.O. Box 1182
Washington, DC 20013
703-385-7565
Provides information and referrals.

Kempe National Center for the
   Prevention and Treatment of
   Child Abuse and Neglect
1205 Oneida Street
Denver, CO 80220
303-321-3963
This organization provides individual and group therapy for victims of child abuse and provides consultations to professionals who work with children.

National Center for Missing and
   Exploited Children
2102 Wilson Blvd., Suite 550
Arlington, VA 22201
1-800-843-5678 (ask for media
   director)

National Committee for
   Prevention of Child Abuse
332 South Michigan Avenue
Suite 1600
Chicago, IL 60604
312-663-3520
This organization provides education and referrals on child abuse.

Parents Anonymous
2230 Hawthorne Blvd., Suite 208
Torrance, CA 90505
1-800-421-0353 (except in CA)
1-800-353-0368 (CA only)
This organization provides parents with group therapy to combat child abuse and serves children from dysfunctional families.

SCAN (Suspected Child Abuse
   and Neglect)
902 High Street
Little Rock, AK 72217
501-372-7226
This organization investigates and works with families of children nine years old and younger who have been physically abused.

Society for the Prevention of
   Cruelty to Children
161 William Street
New York, NY 10003
212-233-5500
This organization provides referrals and counseling to families and children suffering from physical and sexual abuse.

Runaways

National Network of Runaway
   and Youth Services, Inc.
1400 I Street NW
Suite 330
Washington, DC 20005
202-783-7949
This organization provides services for families and youth at risk for child abuse, drug abuse, AIDS, and alcoholism.

The National Runaway
   Switchboard
1-800-621-4000
Runaways receive referrals to hospitals, shelters, and social service agencies. The switchboard also lets runaways and their families leave messages for one another. All calls are confidential.

Sexually Transmitted Diseases

The following organizations can provide information on sexually transmitted diseases, including AIDS, and on safer sex practices.

Centers for Disease Control
  AIDS Hotline
1-800-342-7514

CHOICE Hotline
215-592-0550
This help line answers teenagers' questions about sexually transmitted diseases, AIDS, birth control, pregnancy, and other related topics. Spanish operators available.

Gay Men's Health Crisis Hotline
212-807-6655
Provides information on AIDS.

Suicide

Suicide Hotline Samaritans of
  New York
212-673-3000
This service offers suicide intervention and hospital referrals.

Organizations such as the Federation of Protestant Welfare Agencies, Catholic Charities, or the Jewish Board of Family Services often are listed in the yellow pages under "Social Service Organizations." They can provide information and referrals for families.

For Further Reading

Bingham, Mindy, et al. *Challenges: A Young Man's Journal for Self-Awareness and Personal Planning*, Ed. Barbara Greene and Kathleen Peters. Santa Barbara, Calif.: Advocacy Press, 1984.

Bingham, Mindy; Edmondson, Judy. *Choices: A Teen Woman's Journal for Self-Awareness and Personal Planning*, Ed. Dennis Coon and Sevren Coon. Santa Barbara, Calif.: Advocacy Press, 1983.

Brown, Duane. *Dropping Out or Hanging In*. Chicago: NTC Publishing Group, 1990.

Cohen, Daniel and Susan. *Teenage Competition: A Survival Guide*. New York: M. Evans & Co., 1986.

Eble, Diane; Lutes, Chris; Bearrs, Kris. *Welcome to High School*. New York: Zondervan Publishing Co., 1991.

Featherstone, Bonnie D.; Reilly, Jill M.; Watts, Jean. *College Comes Sooner Than You Think!: The Essential College Planning Guide for High School Students and Their Families.* Cincinnati: Ohio Psychology Press, 1990.

Gordon, Sol. *The Teenage Survival Book.* New York: Times Books, 1981.

Haley, Beverly A. *Focus on School: A Reference Handbook.* Los Angeles: Teenage Perspective Series, 1990.

Heron, Helen H. *College Countdown: Everything You Need to Know for Successful College Application.* Hartford: Edu-Care, 1992.

Levine, M.D., Mel. *Keeping a Head in School: A Student's Book About Learning Abilities and Learning Disorders.* Cambridge: Educators Publishing Service, 1990.

London, Kathleen, with Caparulo, Robert. *Who Am I? Who Are You?* Reading, Mass.: Addison-Wesley, 1983.

Mayer, Barbara. *How to Succeed in High School.* VGM Career Horizons, 1992.

McCoy, Kathy. *Why Am I So Miserable If These Are the Best Years of My Life?* New York: Avon Books, 1981.

Pierce, Olive. *No Easy Roses: A Look at the Lives of City Teenagers.* Olive Pierce Publishing Co., 1986.

Powledge, Fred. *You'll Survive: Late Blooming, Early Blooming, Loneliness, Klutziness, and Other Problems of Adolescence, and How to Live Through Them.* New York: Scribner's Young Readers, 1986.

Roberts, Gail C.; Guttormson, Lorraine; Wallner, Rosemary. *You and School: A Survival Guide for Adolescence* (Self Help for Kids Series). San Francisco: Free Spirit Publishing Co., 1990.

Ryan, Elizabeth A.; Phyllis Steinbrecher. *Getting into the College of Your Choice.* New York: Perigee Books, 1986.

Wesson, Carolyn McClenahan. *Teen Troubles.* New York: Walker Publishing Co., 1988.

Wirths, Gibson; Kruhan, Mary Bowman. *I Hate School: How to Hang In and When to Drop Out.* New York: T.Y. Crowell, 1987.

INDEX